# Cheat Codes and Beast Mode:

# Using Today's Technology to

# Unlock Your Business Potential

*ByTaylor Christensen*

I0477992

In *Cheat Codes and Beast Mode*, learn to navigate and leverage today's most powerful technology tools to revolutionize the way you do business. From mastering data analytics and artificial intelligence to streamlining operations with automation, this book is a practical guide for unlocking the potential hidden in today's digital landscape.

Inside, you'll find:

- **Actionable strategies** to enhance productivity and maximize efficiency
- **Real-world examples** of companies that have transformed their growth trajectories through tech innovation
- **Step-by-step guides** to implementing essential tools that will help you scale faster
- **Expert tips** on adapting to new technologies and staying ahead of competitors

Whether you're a startup founder, an established business owner, or a professional looking to elevate your team, this book will empower you to switch into "Beast Mode" and achieve unprecedented levels of success.

Embrace technology and start using these "cheat codes" today— unlock your business potential and lead your industry into the future!

# Introduction

In today's rapidly evolving world, technology isn't just for tech enthusiasts and software developers. It's for anyone who wants to work smarter, save time, and grow their business. Imagine cutting down hours of work to minutes, reaching more customers than ever before, and making decisions backed by powerful insights—all without having to understand every line of code or technical detail. That's the promise of artificial intelligence (AI) and automated systems, which can help even the least tech-savvy business owners achieve new levels of productivity and success.

If the idea of using AI or automation sounds intimidating, you're not alone. Many people see these tools as complex and out of reach, thinking they require years of technical training or an IT team on standby. But the truth is, modern technology is more accessible than ever, designed to be intuitive, user-friendly, and, most importantly, transformative for businesses of all sizes and backgrounds.

This book is your guide to embracing technology confidently, even if you've never considered yourself "tech-savvy." Together, we'll walk through practical, easy-to-follow steps for using AI and automated systems to streamline tasks, enhance customer experiences, and make data-driven decisions. Whether you're looking to automate your marketing, manage your time more effectively, or use AI to predict what your customers need before they know it themselves, this book will help you unlock the full potential of these tools.

In each chapter of this book, we'll cover the foundational principles of AI and automation in a way that makes sense, even if you're starting from scratch. But theory alone isn't enough to make real change, so we're taking it a step further.

At the end of each chapter, you'll find a special "Get Real" section, where we'll apply the lessons directly to real estate tasks.

These "Get Real" sections are designed to show you how each technology skill or concept can be applied in practical, impactful ways within the real estate world. Whether it's generating leads, automating follow-ups, managing client relationships, or handling documentation, we'll explore how AI and automation can help streamline your workflow, increase your reach, and ultimately grow your business.

By combining tech insights with industry-specific applications, you'll gain a clear understanding of exactly how to put these tools to work. The result? A powerful toolkit that doesn't just teach you about AI and automation but shows you, step by step, how to use them to create real value in your real estate business.

You don't need to be an expert in AI or automation to benefit from them; you just need the right guidance and a willingness to explore new possibilities. So, if you're ready to transform your business, let's get started. Welcome to a journey where technology works for you, not the other way around.

# Chapter 1: Using AI to Generate a Logo, Catchphrase, and Marketing Materials

A brand's image is one of its most powerful assets. Your logo, catchphrase, and marketing materials are often the first things a customer sees, forming their first impression of your business. But creating these from scratch can be time-consuming and expensive, especially if you're starting without a design or marketing team. Here's where AI steps in to help.

In this chapter, we'll explore how to use AI tools to generate a logo, a catchy tagline, and professional-looking marketing materials with minimal cost and effort. You'll learn about user-friendly AI tools that can streamline this process and give your brand a polished, professional look.

## Step 1: Creating a Logo with AI

Your logo represents the essence of your business, making it memorable and recognizable. Using AI-powered logo generators, you can create a logo in just a few minutes by following these steps:

1. **Choose a Logo Generator:** There are several AI logo generators available, such as Looka, LogoMaker, and Tailor Brands. These tools let you input your business name, industry, and preferences, and they generate multiple logo options.
2. **Set Your Style Preferences:** Most tools allow you to choose between different styles (modern, classic, playful, elegant, etc.), colors, and fonts. AI will then use

these inputs to create a logo that aligns with your brand's style.

3. **Customize and Download:** Once AI generates a few logo options, you can edit the designs, colors, and fonts to your liking. When satisfied, download your new logo in multiple formats suitable for websites, social media, and print.

## Step 2: Developing a Catchphrase or Tagline with AI

A great tagline sticks in people's minds, giving them a quick sense of what your brand stands for. If you're struggling to create a catchy slogan, AI-powered tools like ChatGPT or Jasper can help brainstorm ideas:

1. **Define Your Brand Identity:** Start by clarifying your brand's mission, target audience, and core values. The clearer your identity, the better the tagline suggestions will align.
2. **Input Your Requirements:** Use AI tools by giving them prompts, like "Suggest a catchy tagline for a real estate business that emphasizes trust and expertise," and let the tool generate options.
3. **Refine and Select:** You may need to refine the prompt based on the initial output, adding specific words or themes until you get a tagline that feels perfect.

## Step 3: Creating Marketing Materials with AI

From social media graphics to brochures, AI can help you produce professional-looking marketing materials that attract attention and engage customers. Here's how to leverage AI tools for different types of content:

- **Social Media Graphics:** Platforms like Canva and Adobe Express offer AI-powered templates for social media. You can input your logo, colors, and text to generate consistent and eye-catching designs across platforms like Instagram, Facebook, and LinkedIn.

- **Content Creation for Ads and Posts:** AI tools like Copy.ai and Writesonic can generate text for ads, social media posts, and even blog posts. Provide basic information about your product or campaign goals, and these tools will create content that's polished and aligned with your brand voice.
- **Email Templates and Newsletters:** With AI-driven email marketing tools such as Mailchimp and HubSpot, you can create personalized email templates that capture your brand's tone. These tools can suggest subject lines and layouts that increase open rates and engagement.
- **Business Cards and Brochures:** AI-based design platforms can generate business cards, flyers, and brochures that incorporate your logo, colors, and branding. Simply choose a template, add your information, and customize.

## "Get Real" for Real Estate

To bring these concepts to life in real estate, here's how you could use each of these AI-powered tools:

- **Logo Creation:** Design a logo that captures your niche, whether that's luxury homes or eco-friendly properties. Use a sophisticated color palette and sleek fonts to convey trust and professionalism.
- **Catchphrase Creation:** A tagline like "Building Dreams, One Home at a Time" or "Your Partner in Finding Home" could reflect your commitment to helping clients find the right property.
- **Marketing Materials for Listings and Open Houses:** Create professional graphics for social media, such as "New Listing" and "Open House" posts, with AI design tools. You can generate listing descriptions, property highlight flyers, and customer email templates that showcase your expertise and market insights.

## Wrapping Up

This chapter has introduced you to the basics of creating your brand's image with AI tools. With these capabilities, you can give your business a professional, cohesive look that builds trust and recognition. In the next chapter, we'll dive deeper into AI-driven customer relationship management and lead generation tools to build on your marketing foundation and grow your client base.

# Chapter 2: Building Your Website with AI

A website is the cornerstone of your online presence—it's where potential clients learn about your business, browse your services, and contact you. However, designing a professional website can feel overwhelming, especially if you're not familiar with coding or web design. Thankfully, AI has simplified this process, making it possible for anyone to build a beautiful, functional website with minimal effort.

In this chapter, we'll guide you through using AI tools to create a fully customized website. You'll discover how AI can help with everything from layout and design to generating SEO-friendly content that drives traffic to your site.

## Step 1: Choosing an AI Website Builder

AI-powered website builders have revolutionized the process of creating a website. Platforms like Wix ADI (Artificial Design Intelligence), Bookmark, and Zyro allow you to build a complete website in minutes. Here's how to get started:

1. **Select a Platform:** Start by choosing an AI website builder that best suits your needs. For example:
    - **Wix ADI:** This tool is excellent for beginners and allows for extensive customization, making it great for building feature-rich sites.
    - **Bookmark:** Known for its intuitive drag-and-drop interface, Bookmark's AI assistant, AIDA, guides you through every step of the site-building process.

- Zyro: Zyro's AI website builder is straightforward and affordable, perfect for small business owners looking for a quick start.
2. **Input Your Business Information:** AI website builders typically begin by asking a few questions about your business, such as your industry, goals, and the type of website you want to create (e.g., informational, e-commerce, portfolio). Based on your answers, the platform generates a customized layout and design.
3. **Customize the Design:** AI will generate a template tailored to your business's style, but you still have control over layout, colors, fonts, and imagery. Customize these elements to match your brand identity and create a cohesive look.

## Step 2: Creating Website Content with AI

Once the design is set, the next step is to fill your website with engaging, relevant content. For those who struggle with writing or need help creating content quickly, AI content generators like ChatGPT, Writesonic, and Copy.ai are invaluable tools.

1. **Generate Content Ideas:** Use AI to brainstorm ideas for sections like "About Us," "Services," and "Frequently Asked Questions." For example, a prompt like "Write an About Us page for a real estate business focused on luxury properties" will generate a draft for you to refine.
2. **Write SEO-Friendly Copy:** AI content generators can also help you write search engine optimized (SEO) content, which makes it easier for potential customers to find your site. You can ask AI to include relevant keywords or create content that answers common questions in your field to improve visibility.
3. **Create Blog Posts and Articles:** Adding a blog to your website is a great way to attract visitors and establish your expertise. Use AI to draft blog topics, outlines, or even entire posts. For example, you might request content on topics like "Tips for First-Time Homebuyers"

or "What to Look for in a Vacation Home," and AI can provide initial drafts.

## Step 3: Adding Functional Features with AI

A website isn't just a static page; it can be an interactive experience that engages visitors. Here's how AI can help add functional features that improve user experience:

1. **Chatbots for Customer Support:** AI-powered chatbots like those from Tidio or Chatfuel can answer visitor questions in real-time, provide basic customer service, and even guide users to the right pages on your website. This creates an instant support channel for your visitors, increasing engagement and lead generation.
2. **Automated Scheduling Tools:** For service-based businesses, integrating an AI-driven booking tool like Calendly or SimplyBook.me allows visitors to book appointments or consultations directly on your website. This saves time and improves customer convenience.
3. **Personalized Recommendations:** Some AI tools, like Recombee, can suggest relevant products, services, or blog posts to visitors based on their browsing behavior, providing a tailored experience that keeps users on your site longer.
4. **SEO Optimization:** AI tools like Surfer SEO and Semrush can analyze your website's content and provide recommendations to improve its ranking on search engines. These tools suggest keywords, heading structures, and content updates to ensure your website attracts as much organic traffic as possible.

## Step 4: Testing and Launching Your Website

Before launching, it's essential to test your website to ensure it's user-friendly and performs well. Here's how AI can help:

1. **User Experience (UX) Testing:** AI-based UX tools like Hotjar analyze user behavior to identify areas for

improvement. You can see where visitors click, how far they scroll, and where they drop off, allowing you to make data-driven design adjustments.

2. **Performance Optimization:** Tools like PageSpeed Insights can analyze your website's loading time and suggest ways to improve speed, which is essential for user satisfaction and SEO.

3. **A/B Testing:** Platforms like Optimizely use AI to conduct A/B tests on various elements (like headings, colors, or calls-to-action) and recommend adjustments based on user interactions, helping you optimize the website for better conversions.

## "Get Real" for Real Estate

Here's how a real estate business might use these AI-driven features to create a website that converts visitors into clients:

- **Add a Virtual Tour Feature:** Many real estate AI platforms allow for virtual tour integration, offering an immersive experience for potential buyers who can't view properties in person.
- **Real-Time Chat for Client Inquiries:** A chatbot can provide immediate answers to common questions, helping visitors get in touch, schedule showings, or request more information about specific properties.
- **Neighborhood Guides and Blog Content:** Use AI to generate neighborhood guides or blog posts that attract potential buyers and position you as a knowledgeable resource.

## Wrapping Up

By the end of this chapter, you'll have a complete, professional-looking website that serves as a powerful marketing tool for your business. With AI handling much of the heavy lifting, you'll save time and resources while creating a site that reflects your brand and meets your customers' needs.

# Chapter 3: Using AI to Write Product Descriptions

Writing product descriptions that engage customers and encourage them to make a purchase can be challenging, especially if you have numerous products or services to showcase. Effective descriptions are more than just a list of features—they tell a story, highlight benefits, and convey why your product or service is worth buying. With the help of AI, you can streamline this process, generating compelling, SEO-friendly descriptions quickly and consistently.

In this chapter, we'll walk through how AI can assist in writing high-quality product descriptions. You'll discover how to use AI tools to create descriptions that not only captivate potential buyers but also improve search engine visibility.

## Step 1: Selecting the Right AI Tool for Product Descriptions

AI-driven writing tools have been designed to generate persuasive content across industries. Here are some popular options to consider:

- **ChatGPT or Jasper:** Both platforms are versatile and can create descriptions tailored to your brand's tone and audience.
- **Copy.ai and Writesonic:** These tools offer templates specifically for product descriptions, enabling you to get started quickly.
- **Anyword:** Known for its focus on persuasive copy, Anyword can generate data-backed descriptions with

predictive performance scores, which helps you select the most effective phrasing.

## Step 2: Structuring Product Descriptions with AI

The best product descriptions are both informative and engaging, focusing on what the product does for the customer. Here's how to approach structuring your descriptions with AI:

1. **Start with the Basics:** Input your product's name, features, and core benefits into the AI tool. For example, a real estate description might include details about a property's location, square footage, amenities, and key selling points.
2. **Define the Target Audience:** Many AI tools allow you to specify the tone and style of the text. Make sure to select an audience that fits your product—for example, "luxury buyers," "eco-conscious consumers," or "first-time homeowners."
3. **Highlight Benefits Over Features:** To make descriptions compelling, emphasize what the product will do for the buyer. Instead of simply listing features, ask the AI to phrase features as benefits. For example, "spacious living room" becomes "a spacious living room perfect for family gatherings and entertaining guests."
4. **Incorporate a Call-to-Action (CTA):** End each description with a CTA, such as "Schedule a tour today" for real estate, or "Start your journey with this eco-friendly, sustainable option." A strong CTA encourages the reader to take the next step.

## Step 3: Using AI to Optimize Descriptions for SEO

For online sales, visibility is crucial. Optimizing product descriptions for search engines can help your products reach a wider audience. AI can assist by suggesting keywords and structuring descriptions for SEO:

1. **Identify Relevant Keywords:** Many AI writing tools, like Surfer SEO and Semrush, can suggest keywords that are commonly searched for in your industry. Use these keywords naturally in your descriptions to improve search engine rankings.
2. **Add Long-Tail Keywords:** Long-tail keywords, which are more specific phrases (like "luxury condo with ocean view"), often attract customers further along in the buying process. Ask the AI to incorporate these phrases into your descriptions.
3. **Create SEO-Friendly Meta Descriptions:** AI can also generate meta descriptions for your products. Meta descriptions are short summaries that appear in search engine results. A good meta description includes relevant keywords and a brief call-to-action, such as "Discover your dream home with a private garden and modern amenities."

## Step 4: Fine-Tuning and Editing with AI

While AI can generate strong drafts, it's still important to review and edit each description to make sure it aligns with your brand's voice and standards. Here's how to fine-tune AI-generated content:

1. **Adjust for Tone and Style:** Ensure the description matches your brand voice—whether it's formal, conversational, luxurious, or friendly. Use AI tools to modify the tone as needed, or make quick manual edits.
2. **Add Personal Touches:** Include any unique selling points or insider knowledge that might make your product stand out. For example, if you're describing a property in real estate, add unique details about the neighborhood that may appeal to the buyer.
3. **Ensure Consistency Across Descriptions:** For businesses with multiple products, consistency is key. AI can help maintain a similar tone across all descriptions, but a final review will ensure they are consistent and align with your brand's messaging.

## Step 5: Testing and Improving AI-Generated Descriptions

To maximize the effectiveness of your product descriptions, test different versions to see which ones perform best. Here are a few ways to use AI to evaluate and improve your descriptions:

1. **A/B Testing:** Some e-commerce and content platforms allow you to A/B test product descriptions. You can use AI to generate multiple versions of a description, then test which one gets better results in terms of conversions or engagement.
2. **Predictive Performance Analysis:** Certain AI tools, like Anyword, provide predictive scores for different versions of your text, helping you select the version with the best potential performance.
3. **Gather Customer Feedback:** Once your descriptions are live, pay attention to customer feedback and interactions. Use this information to make improvements, and consider using AI again to refine descriptions based on customer interests or inquiries.

## "Get Real" for Real Estate

Here's how a real estate business might use AI to write compelling property descriptions:

- **Highlight Lifestyle Benefits:** For a luxury property, emphasize lifestyle perks. Instead of "large balcony," say "a private balcony offering breathtaking sunset views perfect for unwinding at the end of the day."
- **Generate SEO-Optimized Descriptions:** Tell AI programs to use keywords like "family-friendly neighborhood," "newly renovated," or "close to top-rated schools" to attract buyers searching for these features.
- **Personalized Features:** Include specific details about the property, like "granite countertops in a chef-inspired kitchen" or "spacious walk-in closets," to create a vivid picture.

- **Neighborhood Insights:** Provide a sense of the community by mentioning nearby attractions, parks, or restaurants, helping prospective buyers envision the area as their future home.

## Wrapping Up

By leveraging AI for product descriptions, you'll save time while creating high-quality, engaging content that boosts your business's online visibility and sales potential. AI offers flexibility, efficiency, and even insights into what phrasing works best for engaging customers.

In Chapter 4, we'll explore how AI can improve customer engagement through automated, personalized follow-up messages, turning potential leads into loyal clients.

# Chapter 4: Leveraging AI for Customer Relationship Management (CRM) and Lead Generation

Now that you've set up a strong foundation with your brand assets, website, and product descriptions, it's time to dive into one of the most impactful areas of business growth: managing and nurturing client relationships. Building a loyal client base requires understanding your customers' needs, maintaining consistent communication, and identifying new prospects—all of which can be streamlined with AI-driven customer relationship management (CRM) and lead generation tools.

In this chapter, we'll explore how to use AI to enhance customer interactions, improve client retention, and generate quality leads. By integrating these tools, you can ensure a steady pipeline of clients and effectively manage every stage of the customer journey.

## Step 1: Choosing an AI-Enhanced CRM

An AI-powered CRM system can help you manage customer data, track interactions, and identify patterns that lead to better decision-making. Here are a few CRM platforms with AI features to consider:

- **Salesforce Einstein:** Salesforce's AI-driven CRM offers predictive analytics, lead scoring, and personalized recommendations to help prioritize and nurture leads effectively.

- **HubSpot CRM with AI:** HubSpot's AI tools offer insights on customer behavior, suggesting optimized times for communication, automating follow-ups, and even scoring leads for easier targeting.
- **Zoho CRM with Zia AI:** Zoho's AI assistant, Zia, can analyze sales patterns, predict lead conversions, and offer insights based on customer interactions, helping you optimize your approach.

## Step 2: Automating Lead Generation and Scoring

AI has made it easier than ever to generate high-quality leads by analyzing vast amounts of data and spotting trends that might be missed by manual efforts. Here's how AI can streamline lead generation:

1. **Targeted Outreach:** Use AI to segment your audience and create targeted marketing campaigns. By analyzing customer demographics, purchase history, and behavior, AI can help identify which prospects are most likely to convert.
2. **Lead Scoring:** AI algorithms evaluate lead quality by analyzing behaviors like website visits, email engagement, and social media interactions. High-scoring leads can then be prioritized, allowing you to focus on the prospects most likely to convert.
3. **Predictive Analytics:** Predictive lead scoring tools use historical data to forecast which leads are likely to make a purchase. This helps you plan your outreach and allocate resources more efficiently.

## Step 3: Personalizing Customer Interactions with AI

Personalized communication is essential for building strong customer relationships. AI enables personalization at scale, allowing you to tailor your interactions without dedicating hours to each customer. Here's how to use AI for effective personalization:

1. **Automated Follow-Ups:** CRM platforms with AI can schedule and personalize follow-up emails based on customer behavior, ensuring timely responses that feel tailored and attentive. For instance, if a lead has viewed a particular product or service, the AI can send a targeted follow-up email with relevant information or offers.
2. **Behavioral Analysis for Personalization:** AI analyzes past interactions to recommend the best way to engage each client. For instance, if a customer frequently opens emails in the morning, AI can suggest scheduling future emails at that time for maximum engagement.
3. **Customized Product Recommendations:** Based on browsing history and purchase behavior, AI can suggest products or services tailored to each customer's preferences, enhancing the likelihood of conversion.

## Step 4: Enhancing Customer Support with AI Chatbots

AI-powered chatbots allow you to offer immediate support, answering customer inquiries in real time and even handling routine requests without human intervention. Here's how chatbots can improve customer satisfaction and boost efficiency:

1. **24/7 Availability:** AI chatbots can answer questions and handle basic requests around the clock, ensuring that customers always have access to assistance when they need it.
2. **Qualifying Leads:** Chatbots can ask qualifying questions to determine a visitor's needs, then either handle their request or route them to a sales representative for more in-depth assistance. This way, high-priority leads receive immediate attention.
3. **Enhanced Customer Engagement:** Chatbots can recommend products, guide users through the buying process, and answer frequently asked questions,

creating a more engaging and interactive experience on your website.

## Step 5: Gathering and Analyzing Customer Feedback

Customer feedback is essential for improving products and services. AI can help streamline the collection and analysis of feedback, providing actionable insights to enhance your offerings:

1. **Automated Surveys:** Tools like SurveyMonkey and Qualtrics use AI to generate and analyze customer surveys. AI can identify common themes in feedback, such as recurring issues or suggestions for improvement, helping you prioritize changes.
2. **Sentiment Analysis:** AI sentiment analysis tools analyze customer reviews and social media comments to gauge public perception. This helps you understand how your customers feel about your brand and adjust your strategy accordingly.
3. **Customer Satisfaction Scores:** Some AI-powered CRMs automatically calculate customer satisfaction scores based on recent interactions, providing a quick snapshot of how well you're meeting customer needs.

### "Get Real" for Real Estate

For a real estate business, AI-enhanced CRM and lead generation can be particularly powerful. Here's how these strategies could apply to your field:

- **Lead Scoring for Buyers and Sellers:** Use AI to score leads based on their browsing history, email engagement, or property inquiries. This helps prioritize clients who are more likely to make a transaction.
- **Personalized Listings:** AI can recommend properties based on each client's preferences and browsing

history, enhancing the customer experience and keeping them engaged with your offerings.

- **Automated Follow-Ups for Property Visits:** Schedule automated follow-ups after property tours or inquiries, providing additional information or scheduling options to keep the momentum going.
- **Sentiment Analysis for Client Feedback:** Gather insights from client reviews and testimonials, identifying areas where your services excel or may need improvement.

## Wrapping Up

By integrating AI-driven CRM and lead generation tools into your business, you're creating a system that builds relationships, nurtures leads, and increases conversions—all while saving time and resources. Whether it's automating follow-ups, scoring leads, or personalizing outreach, AI can transform the way you manage and grow your client base, freeing you to focus on building lasting connections with your clients.

In Chapter 6, we'll explore how AI can assist with data analysis and decision-making, helping you make informed business choices based on insights gathered from customer behavior and market trends.

# Chapter 5: Data Analysis and Informed Decision-Making

Once your customer relationships and lead generation processes are streamlined, the next step is making data-driven decisions to optimize business performance. AI-driven data analysis tools offer powerful insights into customer behavior, industry trends, and internal operations. With the right insights, you can refine your strategies, improve customer experiences, and increase profitability.

In this chapter, we'll explore how to use AI for data analysis and business intelligence. You'll learn how AI can turn raw data into actionable insights, giving you a competitive edge in a rapidly evolving market.

## Step 1: Choosing the Right AI-Powered Data Analysis Tools

There are various AI data analysis tools tailored for businesses of all sizes. Here's a quick look at some popular options:

- **Google Analytics with AI Insights:** Google Analytics leverages machine learning to provide insights into website traffic, audience demographics, and behavior patterns. Its AI-driven insights suggest areas for improvement in engagement and marketing.
- **Tableau with Einstein AI:** Tableau's integration with Salesforce Einstein AI allows for predictive analytics, trend forecasting, and visual data representation.
- **Microsoft Power BI with AI Capabilities:** Power BI's AI features include visual recognition, natural language processing (NLP), and custom machine learning

models, making it versatile for analyzing complex datasets.

## Step 2: Identifying Key Metrics for Data Analysis

For AI data analysis to be effective, you'll need to identify the key metrics that align with your business objectives. Here are some common metrics across industries:

1. **Customer Behavior Metrics:** AI can analyze metrics such as average purchase value, customer retention rate, and customer lifetime value, providing a clear picture of buying behaviors and trends.
2. **Marketing Metrics:** AI helps analyze conversion rates, cost per acquisition, and return on ad spend, allowing you to assess the effectiveness of marketing efforts.
3. **Operational Efficiency Metrics:** For internal operations, metrics such as time-to-completion, production costs, and inventory turnover can reveal inefficiencies and opportunities for cost savings.

By focusing on metrics aligned with your goals, AI can provide targeted insights that drive real change.

## Step 3: Using Predictive Analytics to Forecast Trends

AI's predictive analytics capabilities go beyond identifying current trends; they can also forecast future patterns based on historical data. Here's how AI can help with business forecasting:

1. **Sales Forecasting:** AI can analyze past sales data to predict future revenue, helping you prepare for demand fluctuations and seasonal trends.
2. **Customer Retention Prediction:** By identifying patterns in customer behavior, AI can forecast which clients are likely to remain loyal and which are at risk of

churning. This insight allows you to proactively engage and retain valuable customers.

3. **Market Trend Analysis:** AI tools analyze external data sources, such as social media trends, news, and economic data, to identify emerging market trends. This can guide your product or service offerings to align with current demand.

## Step 4: Leveraging Real-Time Analytics for Immediate Decisions

AI-powered real-time analytics allow you to make on-the-spot decisions based on current data. This is especially valuable in fast-paced industries where timing is critical:

1. **Customer Support:** Real-time analytics can alert your team to spikes in customer inquiries or complaints, allowing you to address issues proactively and improve customer satisfaction.
2. **Inventory Management:** For businesses managing physical products, AI can monitor inventory levels in real time and suggest restocking when supplies are low. This ensures you meet demand without overstocking.
3. **Social Media Monitoring:** AI-driven social listening tools track brand mentions and sentiment on social media, enabling you to respond to public sentiment quickly and effectively.

## Step 5: Visualizing Data for Clear Insights

AI-enhanced data visualization tools turn complex datasets into easy-to-understand visuals, making it simpler to spot trends and communicate findings:

1. **Data Dashboards:** Tools like Tableau and Power BI allow you to create customizable dashboards that display real-time insights. Dashboards can help team members across departments make informed decisions based on the latest data.

2. **Interactive Reports:** Interactive visuals such as heat maps, trend lines, and scatter plots make it easier to see patterns and relationships within data. AI-driven recommendations can even highlight unusual trends or correlations worth investigating further.
3. **Natural Language Summaries:** Some AI tools can generate plain-language summaries of complex data, making it accessible to team members who may not be data experts. This promotes data-driven decision-making across the organization.

## "Get Real" for Real Estate

Here's how a real estate business might use AI data analysis to gain valuable insights:

- **Analyzing Buyer Trends:** AI can identify buyer preferences, such as popular property types, locations, or amenities, helping you focus your listings and marketing efforts.
- **Predicting Property Value Changes:** Predictive analytics can forecast market changes and property values, guiding investment decisions for clients and positioning your agency as a knowledgeable resource.
- **Customer Behavior Tracking:** AI can segment clients based on their browsing history, inquiries, and previous purchases, allowing you to tailor follow-up communication and recommendations.
- **Performance Tracking for Agents:** Use AI to analyze agent performance metrics, such as sales volume, customer satisfaction, and average time to close, and make data-driven decisions for team development and training.

## Wrapping Up

Incorporating AI-driven data analysis into your business strategy allows you to make informed, strategic decisions based on real-time and predictive insights. By understanding customer behaviors, forecasting trends, and monitoring performance, AI empowers you to stay agile in a competitive market.

In Chapter 5, we'll explore how AI can enhance customer engagement through personalized email campaigns and targeted messaging, helping you convert leads and nurture client relationships further.

# Chapter 6: Enhancing Customer Engagement with AI-Driven Email Campaigns and Targeted Messaging

Engaging with customers in meaningful ways is essential for building long-term loyalty and increasing conversion rates. However, reaching the right people with the right message at the right time can be challenging, especially as your client base grows. AI can transform customer engagement by personalizing communication, automating follow-ups, and analyzing campaign performance to help you refine your approach.

In this chapter, we'll explore how AI can elevate your email marketing and messaging strategies, enabling you to connect with clients on a deeper level and boost engagement. Whether you're nurturing leads or re-engaging existing customers, AI-driven email campaigns and targeted messaging allow you to communicate more effectively.

## Step 1: Choosing an AI-Powered Email Marketing Platform

Several email marketing platforms offer AI-driven features that streamline and enhance your campaigns. Here are a few popular options:

- **Mailchimp with Smart Recommendations:** Mailchimp uses AI to suggest optimal times to send emails, recommend audience segments, and personalize email content for each recipient.

- **ActiveCampaign with Machine Learning Insights:** ActiveCampaign's AI tools provide predictive sending, advanced segmentation, and personalized content recommendations.
- **HubSpot with AI Personalization:** HubSpot's AI tools focus on content personalization, A/B testing, and behavior-based triggers to help you optimize your email campaigns.

## Step 2: Segmenting Your Audience with AI

Audience segmentation is essential for delivering relevant content, and AI makes this process more precise and scalable. Here's how AI can help:

1. **Behavioral Segmentation:** AI analyzes customers' past interactions with your business, such as purchases, website visits, and email engagement, to create segments based on behavior. For example, you can identify groups like "frequent buyers," "new leads," or "dormant customers."
2. **Predictive Segmentation:** Predictive AI models analyze data to group customers based on their likelihood to convert, engage, or churn. By targeting high-probability segments, you can allocate resources more effectively and increase your chances of successful engagement.
3. **Demographic and Psychographic Segmentation:** AI can combine demographic data (age, location, income) with psychographic data (interests, values) to create highly targeted segments. This allows you to tailor messages for different customer personas.

## Step 3: Personalizing Email Content with AI

Personalized emails are far more effective than generic ones, and AI enables you to take personalization to a new level. Here's how to create personalized content that resonates:

1. **Dynamic Content Blocks:** AI-powered platforms allow you to create dynamic content blocks that adjust based on the recipient's profile. For instance, an email could automatically display different images or text depending on the reader's interests or past behavior.
2. **Product Recommendations:** AI can analyze customer preferences to suggest products or services that are relevant to each recipient. For example, if a client recently toured properties with a garden, your email can highlight similar listings.
3. **Personalized Subject Lines and Greetings:** AI can generate personalized subject lines and greetings based on the recipient's name, location, or recent interactions. These small touches can significantly increase open and click-through rates.

## Step 4: Optimizing Send Times and Frequency with Predictive Analytics

The timing and frequency of your emails can make a big difference in engagement rates. AI-driven platforms offer tools to optimize your sending strategy:

1. **Predictive Send Times:** AI analyzes each recipient's past behavior to determine the best time to send an email. By sending emails when customers are most likely to check their inbox, you increase the chances of engagement.
2. **Frequency Optimization:** AI can identify the ideal frequency for each customer based on their response history. This prevents oversending to customers who prefer less frequent emails and ensures that more engaged customers receive regular updates.
3. **Automated Follow-Up Sequences:** AI can trigger automated follow-up sequences based on customer

actions. For instance, if a recipient clicks a link to view a property listing, the AI can schedule a follow-up email with similar properties or a prompt to schedule a tour.

## Step 5: Analyzing Campaign Performance with AI

Tracking the success of your campaigns is crucial to refining your approach. AI can provide detailed insights and recommendations to help you continuously improve:

1. **A/B Testing with AI Insights:** Many platforms allow you to run A/B tests on different versions of an email, such as subject lines, images, or CTAs. AI can help you interpret the results, suggesting which elements were most effective and recommending improvements for future campaigns.
2. **Customer Engagement Scoring:** AI tools can assign engagement scores to recipients based on their interactions with your emails. This allows you to prioritize high-scoring customers and re-engage lower-scoring ones with different approaches.
3. **Sentiment Analysis:** AI can analyze the language customers use when they respond to your emails or provide feedback. This helps you gauge the overall sentiment toward your campaigns and adjust the tone and content accordingly.

## "Get Real" for Real Estate

In real estate, personalized email campaigns and targeted messaging can be highly effective in driving engagement. Here's how these strategies could apply:

- **Property Recommendation Emails:** AI can analyze a client's previous searches or property views to recommend similar listings. For example, if a client is interested in properties with waterfront views, you can automatically send them listings that meet this preference.

- **Neighborhood Guides and Market Updates:** Create targeted content like neighborhood guides or real estate market updates, tailored to clients based on their location or interests.
- **Follow-Up After Showings:** AI can automate follow-ups after property showings, sending information on similar properties, financing options, or scheduling additional tours. This keeps clients engaged and helps you move them closer to a purchase decision.
- **Personalized Subject Lines and Greetings:** Use AI to personalize each email with specific details about the property, neighborhood, or recent interactions, increasing the likelihood of the client engaging with the content.

## Wrapping Up

AI-powered email campaigns and targeted messaging help you connect with clients on a more personal level, improving open rates, engagement, and conversions. By tailoring your content, optimizing timing, and analyzing results, you can build stronger relationships with customers and nurture leads through each stage of the journey.

In Chapter 7, we'll discuss how AI can support social media marketing, helping you expand your reach, engage followers, and analyze performance across multiple platforms. This will enable you to build a consistent, impactful online presence that aligns with your business goals.

# Chapter 7: Enhancing Social Media Marketing with AI

Social media has become a cornerstone of modern marketing, allowing businesses to connect with customers, build brand awareness, and engage with audiences worldwide. However, effectively managing multiple social platforms, creating engaging content, and analyzing results can be overwhelming. This is where AI steps in to streamline social media efforts, making it easier to expand your reach, engage followers, and drive consistent growth.

In this chapter, we'll explore how AI can enhance your social media strategy, from content creation and scheduling to performance analysis. With AI-powered tools, you can build a strong online presence that resonates with your target audience and supports your business goals.

## Step 1: Using AI for Content Creation and Curation

AI tools can simplify the process of creating and curating content, helping you maintain an active social media presence with less effort:

1. **Automated Content Suggestions:** AI can analyze popular trends in your industry and suggest content topics that are likely to engage your audience. This helps ensure your posts are relevant and timely.
2. **Image and Video Generation:** AI tools like Canva and Lumen5 can assist in creating high-quality visuals and videos, which are essential for grabbing attention on

social media. Some tools can even convert blog posts into videos or infographics, maximizing content repurposing.

3. **Content Curation:** AI-powered platforms can pull relevant articles, videos, or infographics from around the web, allowing you to share valuable content with your audience without needing to create everything from scratch.

## Step 2: Optimizing Post Timing and Frequency with AI

AI tools analyze audience behavior to determine the best times to post content, ensuring maximum visibility and engagement:

1. **Best Time Recommendations:** AI-driven social media platforms, like Buffer and Hootsuite, offer recommendations on optimal posting times based on when your audience is most active.
2. **Frequency Optimization:** AI can help determine the right posting frequency for each platform, ensuring you post often enough to stay visible without overwhelming your followers.
3. **Automated Scheduling:** Tools like Later and Sprout Social allow you to plan and schedule posts in advance, giving you a consistent online presence even when you're busy with other tasks.

## Step 3: Engaging Followers with AI-Powered Interactions

AI can help you create a more interactive social media presence, engaging with followers in real time and fostering stronger connections:

1. **AI Chatbots for Messaging:** Many platforms now support AI chatbots that can answer basic questions, provide information, or direct users to additional

resources. This is especially useful for customer service on platforms like Facebook and Instagram.

2. **Auto-Responses for Comments and Messages:** AI can recognize common inquiries in comments and messages and provide instant, automated replies, keeping engagement high without requiring constant manual input.

3. **Sentiment Analysis for Engagement:** AI-driven sentiment analysis tools can monitor public reactions to your posts, helping you gauge the mood of your audience. This allows you to address negative feedback promptly or amplify positive interactions.

## Step 4: Analyzing Social Media Performance with AI

AI-powered analytics tools provide in-depth insights into your social media performance, helping you understand what works and what doesn't:

1. **Engagement Tracking:** AI can track engagement metrics such as likes, comments, shares, and clicks across all platforms. This data helps identify which content resonates best with your audience.

2. **Follower Growth Analysis:** AI tools analyze follower growth trends, helping you understand which campaigns or posts attract new followers and how to sustain growth.

3. **Predictive Analytics for Trend Forecasting:** Some AI tools offer predictive analytics, which forecast future performance based on past data. This can help you plan campaigns around anticipated trends, maximizing engagement.

## Step 5: Social Listening with AI

Social listening involves monitoring what people say about your brand or industry online. AI-powered social listening tools provide valuable insights into public sentiment and emerging trends:

1. **Brand Monitoring:** AI tracks mentions of your brand across social media, alerting you to positive or negative mentions so you can engage or respond as needed.
2. **Competitive Analysis:** AI tools can also monitor your competitors' social media activity, providing insights into their strategies and helping you stay competitive.
3. **Trend Spotting:** AI can identify trending topics, hashtags, and conversations relevant to your industry, allowing you to join the conversation early and stay relevant to your audience.

## "Get Real" for Real Estate

For real estate, AI-powered social media marketing can be particularly effective. Here's how these strategies might apply:

- **Property Showcase Content:** Use AI tools to create visually appealing posts showcasing your property listings. AI can suggest the best times to post, maximizing visibility when your audience is most active.
- **Market Trend Updates:** AI can help you curate or generate content related to real estate market trends, neighborhood spotlights, and property investment tips, positioning you as an industry authority.
- **Automated Responses for Inquiries:** AI chatbots can handle basic inquiries about listings or schedule viewings, providing immediate responses and boosting customer satisfaction.
- **Competitive Analysis in Your Area:** AI-driven social listening can track competing real estate agents in your area, giving you insights into successful campaigns and market dynamics.

## Wrapping Up

AI-powered tools for social media allow you to build a consistent, engaging online presence without the need for extensive manual effort. By leveraging AI for content creation, audience engagement, performance analysis, and trend tracking, you can strengthen your brand and increase visibility across social platforms.

In Chapter 8, we'll explore how AI can assist with inventory management and logistics for product-based businesses, helping streamline operations, reduce costs, and ensure products are always available when customers need them.

# Chapter 8: Streamlining Inventory Management and Logistics with AI

For product-based businesses, managing inventory and logistics is critical to maintaining efficient operations and meeting customer demand. However, without the right systems in place, businesses can face stockouts, overstocking, delayed shipments, and high operational costs. This is where AI-driven tools come in—helping businesses forecast demand, optimize inventory, and automate logistics to ensure timely deliveries.

In this chapter, we'll explore how AI can transform inventory management and logistics for your business. With AI, you can make smarter decisions, reduce waste, and ensure your products are always available when customers need them, ultimately improving your bottom line.

## Step 1: AI-Powered Demand Forecasting

Accurate demand forecasting is the foundation of effective inventory management. AI uses historical sales data, market trends, and external factors (like seasonality or economic shifts) to predict future demand more accurately than traditional methods.

1. **Predictive Analytics for Demand Trends:** AI tools analyze past sales data to forecast demand for specific products. This helps ensure you have the right amount of stock at the right time, minimizing both overstocking and stockouts.
2. **Seasonal and Trend Analysis:** AI considers seasonal fluctuations and trends to anticipate product demand. For example, AI can predict higher demand for certain

items during holidays or special events, allowing you to adjust inventory levels in advance.

3. **Real-Time Data Integration:** AI tools integrate with your sales data, monitoring trends in real time. This allows for continuous adjustments to your forecasts, ensuring that inventory decisions are always based on the latest information.

## Step 2: Optimizing Inventory Levels with AI

AI can help you maintain the perfect balance between inventory levels and demand, minimizing waste and ensuring you don't run out of stock.

1. **Automatic Replenishment:** AI tools can track inventory levels and automatically reorder products when stock is low. This helps prevent stockouts and ensures that you never have to rush to replenish products last minute.
2. **Smart Stocking Strategies:** AI can optimize the amount of stock for each product based on demand forecasts. For example, if a product is trending, AI may recommend increasing its stock, whereas products with lower demand may be ordered in smaller quantities.
3. **Stock Rotation and Shelf Management:** AI-powered systems can track product shelf life and suggest which products to sell first, reducing the risk of expired or obsolete inventory.

## Step 3: AI in Warehouse Management

Efficient warehouse management is key to reducing logistics costs and ensuring timely deliveries. AI can help streamline warehouse operations in various ways:

1. **Optimizing Warehouse Layout:** AI analyzes product movement and suggests optimal warehouse layouts to minimize the time spent locating and picking items. This can significantly reduce labor costs and improve fulfillment speed.

2. **Robotic Process Automation (RPA):** In warehouses, AI-powered robots can autonomously pick, pack, and move products. This increases efficiency, reduces human error, and speeds up the entire process from order fulfillment to shipping.
3. **Real-Time Inventory Tracking:** AI-based systems track inventory in real time, helping you avoid discrepancies between physical stock and recorded stock. This helps reduce errors and improve inventory accuracy.

## Step 4: AI-Powered Logistics and Shipping Optimization

Logistics is another area where AI can deliver significant value by optimizing shipping routes, reducing delivery times, and lowering costs.

1. **Route Optimization:** AI-powered logistics software analyzes shipping data to determine the most efficient delivery routes. By factoring in traffic, weather, and delivery schedules, AI can reduce fuel consumption, delivery time, and costs.
2. **Predictive Delivery Estimates:** AI can predict delivery times more accurately based on historical data, weather conditions, and real-time traffic updates. This allows businesses to provide customers with precise delivery windows and improve satisfaction.
3. **Shipment Tracking and Alerts:** AI tools can track shipments and send real-time updates to both you and your customers. If a delivery is delayed, AI can automatically reroute the shipment or notify customers with updated timelines.

## Step 5: AI for Supplier and Vendor Management

AI tools also help streamline supplier and vendor management, ensuring you have reliable sources for your products and that orders are fulfilled on time.

1. **Supplier Performance Tracking:** AI can analyze supplier performance data to identify trends in delivery times, quality, and pricing. This helps you choose the best suppliers and negotiate better terms.
2. **AI-Powered Sourcing Decisions:** AI can analyze market conditions, pricing trends, and availability to recommend the best time to order products from suppliers. This helps you save on costs while ensuring stock levels are maintained.
3. **Risk Management:** AI can identify potential risks in your supply chain, such as supplier delays or geopolitical issues, and provide alternative sourcing options to mitigate these risks.

## Step 6: Real-Time Analytics and Continuous Improvement

One of the biggest benefits of AI in inventory management and logistics is its ability to provide real-time analytics. This data helps businesses continually refine their processes for better efficiency and profitability.

1. **Inventory Turnover Analysis:** AI tools analyze the rate at which products are sold and replenished, providing insights into product performance and inventory turnover. This helps businesses make better decisions about product pricing and inventory levels.
2. **Supply Chain Performance Monitoring:** AI continuously monitors your supply chain, identifying inefficiencies, delays, or disruptions. This allows you to take corrective action quickly, ensuring smooth operations.
3. **Actionable Insights for Improvement:** AI generates reports that highlight areas for improvement in your inventory and logistics operations. These reports can suggest process optimizations, cost reductions, and inventory strategies for better overall performance.

## "Get Real" for Real Estate

For real estate businesses, AI-powered inventory and logistics management can be adapted to streamline processes:

- **Property Inventory Management:** AI can help track and manage your real estate listings, ensuring that you always have an up-to-date inventory of properties available for clients. Predictive analytics can also help you determine the right number of properties to list based on demand in certain areas.
- **Optimizing Property Tours:** AI can suggest optimal schedules and routes for property showings based on location, availability, and client preferences. This helps streamline the process and ensures a seamless experience for your clients.
- **Supplier and Vendor Management for Renovations:** AI can optimize the procurement of materials and services needed for property renovations or maintenance, ensuring that you have everything on hand when you need it and avoiding unnecessary delays.

## Wrapping Up

AI can revolutionize how you manage inventory, track shipments, and handle supplier relationships. By optimizing demand forecasting, automating stock replenishment, and streamlining logistics, AI helps ensure that your products or services are always available when customers need them, while reducing operational costs.

In the next chapter, we'll explore how AI can support financial management, helping you optimize cash flow, forecast expenses, and make data-driven financial decisions to keep your business on track.

# Chapter 9: Utilizing AI for Financial Management

Effective financial management is crucial to the success of any business. Whether you're looking to optimize cash flow, predict future expenses, or make smarter financial decisions, the ability to process and analyze financial data in real-time is essential. Traditional financial management methods can be time-consuming and prone to error, but with AI, businesses can streamline their financial processes, make data-driven decisions, and maintain healthier cash flow.

In this chapter, we'll explore how AI can transform your financial management practices. From automating accounting tasks to providing deep insights into your financial health, AI empowers business owners to manage finances with greater accuracy and efficiency, giving you more time to focus on strategic growth.

## Step 1: Automating Routine Financial Tasks

AI can automate several routine financial tasks, significantly reducing the time and effort spent on manual accounting work:

1. **Invoice Creation and Processing:** AI-powered tools like QuickBooks and Xero can automatically generate invoices based on your sales data and track payments. They can also follow up with clients for overdue payments, reducing the need for manual invoicing and collections.

2. **Expense Categorization:** AI can scan receipts and categorize expenses automatically, saving you time on organizing and inputting transactions. This helps ensure accurate financial records and simplifies tax preparation.
3. **Payroll Automation:** AI tools can automate payroll calculations, tax deductions, and benefits administration, ensuring timely and accurate payments to employees without manual intervention.

## Step 2: Optimizing Cash Flow with AI

Managing cash flow is vital for keeping your business running smoothly. AI can help you monitor and optimize your cash flow in real-time:

1. **Cash Flow Forecasting:** AI uses historical financial data, sales trends, and market conditions to predict cash flow and identify potential shortfalls. By providing accurate forecasts, AI helps you plan ahead and avoid liquidity problems.
2. **Smart Expense Management:** AI analyzes your spending patterns and provides recommendations for reducing costs or reallocating funds more efficiently. It can identify areas where you're overspending and suggest ways to cut unnecessary expenses.
3. **Automated Payment Reminders:** AI can send automated payment reminders to customers, ensuring timely collections and preventing late payments from impacting your cash flow.

## Step 3: AI-Powered Financial Analytics

AI-driven analytics provide deep insights into your financial data, helping you make informed decisions based on real-time information:

1. **Profit and Loss Analysis:** AI can automatically generate profit and loss statements, comparing your

income against expenses and identifying trends. This allows you to spot potential issues early and take corrective action.

2. **Financial Health Monitoring:** AI tools can assess key financial metrics like gross margin, net income, and return on investment (ROI). This helps you monitor your business's financial health and set appropriate benchmarks for growth.

3. **Custom Financial Dashboards:** AI platforms offer customizable dashboards that aggregate financial data into easy-to-read visuals. These dashboards help you track key performance indicators (KPIs) and make data-driven decisions on investments, pricing, and cost-cutting strategies.

## Step 4: AI for Expense Forecasting and Budgeting

AI can help you forecast expenses more accurately, allowing for more precise budgeting:

1. **Predictive Expense Forecasting:** AI analyzes your historical spending data and external factors like market conditions to predict upcoming expenses. This allows you to prepare for large expenses and allocate funds accordingly.

2. **Budget Optimization:** AI-powered tools can suggest optimal budget allocations based on your past financial behavior. Whether it's increasing the marketing budget during peak seasons or reducing overhead costs during slower periods, AI ensures your budget is aligned with business needs.

3. **Scenario Planning:** AI can model different financial scenarios based on variables such as sales growth, economic conditions, or changes in operating costs. This allows you to see how different scenarios might affect your cash flow and plan accordingly.

## Step 5: Enhancing Financial Decision-Making with AI

AI can improve financial decision-making by providing insights that human analysis may miss:

1. **Investment Recommendations:** AI tools can analyze market trends and identify investment opportunities that align with your business goals. They can recommend asset classes or strategies based on your risk tolerance and financial goals.
2. **Credit Risk Assessment:** AI can assess the creditworthiness of potential customers or vendors by analyzing their financial history and market behavior. This helps you make informed decisions about extending credit or entering partnerships.
3. **Tax Optimization:** AI can help you navigate tax laws and regulations by identifying potential deductions, credits, and tax-saving strategies. By optimizing your tax strategy, AI can help you retain more earnings and reduce your overall tax liability.

## Step 6: Fraud Detection and Risk Management

AI can also help safeguard your business from financial fraud and reduce risk:

1. **Fraud Detection Algorithms:** AI can detect unusual patterns in financial transactions, such as unauthorized payments or anomalous spending, and alert you in real time. By proactively identifying potential fraud, you can reduce the likelihood of financial losses.
2. **Risk Assessment Models:** AI can assess the financial risks associated with specific business decisions, such as expanding into a new market or taking on a new client. By evaluating historical data and external conditions, AI helps you make more informed decisions with lower risks.
3. **Regulatory Compliance:** AI tools help ensure compliance with financial regulations by continuously monitoring transactions and financial reporting

requirements. This reduces the risk of fines or legal issues due to non-compliance.

## "Get Real" for Real Estate

For real estate businesses, AI can provide significant advantages in managing finances:

- **Cash Flow and Investment Property Analysis:** AI can help real estate investors forecast cash flow for rental properties, taking into account variables like occupancy rates, property management costs, and local market conditions. This allows you to make smarter decisions about which properties to invest in.
- **Expense Forecasting for Renovations:** If you're managing a property renovation, AI can help forecast renovation costs based on past projects, market prices for materials, and contractor fees. This ensures you stay within budget and avoid unexpected expenses.
- **Optimizing Commissions and Fees:** AI can help you optimize commission structures, taking into account market trends and competitor pricing, to ensure you're charging competitive yet profitable rates for services like property sales and rentals.
- **Loan and Mortgage Management:** AI can help analyze loan options, interest rates, and potential tax impacts, allowing you to make informed decisions about financing real estate transactions or investments.

## Wrapping Up

AI-powered financial management tools can significantly improve the way you manage your business's finances. From automating routine tasks and optimizing cash flow to providing predictive insights and managing risks, AI enables you to make smarter, more informed financial decisions that keep your business on track.

In Chapter 10, we'll explore how AI can support business operations and project management, helping you streamline workflows, improve collaboration, and ensure that tasks are completed on time and within budget.

# Chapter 10: Using AI for Business Operations and Project Management

Managing business operations and projects efficiently is crucial for maintaining productivity and achieving long-term success. However, without the right tools, tasks can slip through the cracks, deadlines may be missed, and team collaboration can suffer. AI-powered solutions can address these challenges, providing businesses with smarter ways to manage workflows, track progress, and ensure that projects stay on track.

In this chapter, we'll explore how AI can support your business operations and project management efforts, helping you streamline tasks, improve communication, and manage resources more effectively. By integrating AI into your day-to-day operations, you can enhance your team's efficiency and reduce the risk of costly errors or delays.

## Step 1: Automating Workflow and Task Management

AI can help automate and organize your daily operations, saving you time and ensuring that tasks are handled efficiently:

1. **Automated Task Assignment:** AI tools like Trello, Asana, and Monday.com can automatically assign tasks based on team members' availability, skill sets, and

workload. This helps ensure that no one is overloaded and that work is evenly distributed.

2. **Smart Task Prioritization:** AI can analyze project timelines, deadlines, and dependencies to suggest which tasks should be prioritized. This ensures that high-priority tasks are addressed first, preventing delays in the overall project timeline.

3. **Task Tracking and Notifications:** AI-powered platforms can track the status of tasks in real time, sending automatic reminders and alerts to team members when deadlines are approaching or when tasks require attention. This helps everyone stay on top of their responsibilities and avoids unnecessary bottlenecks.

## Step 2: Enhancing Collaboration with AI Tools

AI can improve communication and collaboration within your team, ensuring that information is shared seamlessly and everyone stays aligned:

1. **AI-Powered Communication Tools:** Tools like Slack, Microsoft Teams, and Zoom integrate AI to assist with scheduling meetings, managing notifications, and organizing discussions. AI bots can even summarize key points from meetings or conversations, ensuring that all team members are on the same page.

2. **Document Collaboration:** AI-driven platforms like Google Workspace and Notion allow teams to collaborate on documents and presentations in real-time. AI can assist by suggesting edits, organizing content, and even generating reports or summaries to save time.

3. **Automated Meeting Scheduling:** AI-powered schedulers, such as Calendly, can automatically find mutually available times for meetings, reducing the time spent coordinating schedules and ensuring that meetings happen at the most convenient times for all team members.

## Step 3: AI in Project Planning and Resource Management

AI can optimize how you plan and allocate resources, helping you stay within budget and deliver projects on time:

1. **Project Timeline Forecasting:** AI tools can help you develop project timelines by analyzing past projects and considering factors like task dependencies, team availability, and resource requirements. AI then predicts realistic deadlines and milestones to keep the project on track.
2. **Resource Allocation:** AI can assist with resource allocation by analyzing workload data and ensuring that resources (whether human, financial, or equipment) are distributed optimally. This reduces the risk of overburdening certain team members or underutilizing others.
3. **Cost Management and Budgeting:** AI tools can track project costs in real-time, helping you stay within budget by forecasting expenses and identifying potential cost overruns early. AI can also suggest ways to reduce costs, such as adjusting project scope or reallocating resources.

## Step 4: Real-Time Data Analysis and Performance Tracking

AI-powered platforms provide deep insights into your project's performance, helping you make data-driven decisions and adjust strategies as needed:

1. **Project Progress Tracking:** AI tools like Wrike or Basecamp allow you to monitor progress in real time, providing detailed insights into completed tasks, project stages, and upcoming deadlines. These platforms offer visual reports, such as Gantt charts or Kanban boards, that track milestones and show team progress.

2. **Predictive Analytics for Delays:** AI can analyze historical data and detect patterns that may indicate a risk of delays or bottlenecks. For example, if certain tasks are consistently delayed or teams are struggling to meet deadlines, AI can alert you early, enabling you to take corrective action before the project falls behind.
3. **Key Performance Indicators (KPIs):** AI can track and analyze KPIs in real time, such as task completion rates, cost per task, and resource usage. This provides actionable insights into project performance, helping you identify areas that need attention and improve efficiency.

## Step 5: Risk Management and Issue Resolution

AI can proactively identify and mitigate risks, ensuring that projects stay on track and within scope:

1. **Risk Identification:** AI can analyze past projects and current project data to identify potential risks. For example, it may spot issues with resource availability, budget constraints, or customer satisfaction based on patterns observed in previous projects.
2. **Automated Problem Solving:** AI-driven project management systems can suggest solutions to common issues. For example, if a task is delayed, AI can recommend which team members might be available to speed things up or suggest which resources should be reallocated to get back on track.
3. **Scenario Planning:** AI tools can run simulations to model different scenarios and their potential impact on your project. This allows you to assess how changes in resources, timelines, or budgets will affect your project and make adjustments before issues arise.

## Step 6: Continuous Improvement and Post-Project Analysis

After a project is completed, AI can help you analyze performance and identify areas for improvement in future projects:

1. **Post-Project Reviews:** AI can generate reports summarizing project outcomes, including time spent on tasks, budget adherence, and overall team performance. These insights help you learn from past projects and apply those lessons to future work.
2. **Continuous Learning:** AI-powered systems learn from each project they manage, continuously improving their suggestions and recommendations for future tasks. As you use AI tools more, they become better at predicting needs and automating processes to save time.
3. **Customer Feedback Analysis:** AI can also analyze customer feedback on completed projects, providing insights into how well the project met client expectations and where improvements are needed. This feedback is valuable for refining processes and enhancing client satisfaction in future projects.

## "Get Real" for Real Estate

For real estate businesses, AI-powered project management can be a game-changer:

- **Managing Property Renovations:** AI can help you manage property renovation projects by forecasting costs, tracking contractor progress, and ensuring that tasks are completed on schedule. AI tools can also help prioritize renovations based on market demand or client preferences.
- **Scheduling Property Showings:** AI can automate the scheduling of property showings for clients, aligning the availability of agents, clients, and properties. It can also send automatic reminders to clients, ensuring they don't miss their appointments.
- **Streamlining Property Listings:** AI tools can track which properties are getting the most interest and suggest which listings need to be promoted more.

Additionally, AI can help track leads, assign them to the right team members, and follow up with potential buyers automatically.

- **Team Collaboration:** Real estate teams often need to collaborate across different tasks, from listing properties to managing closings. AI can help by streamlining communication, assigning tasks to agents, and tracking the status of each deal in real time.

## Wrapping Up

AI-powered tools for business operations and project management can save you time, improve efficiency, and reduce errors. By automating routine tasks, optimizing resource allocation, and providing valuable insights, AI helps you keep projects on track and within budget, ensuring timely delivery and client satisfaction.

From now on we will focus on how to use automated programs to complete tasks.

# Chapter 11: Using Bot Programs for Text Messaging in Your CRM

Effective communication with clients is at the heart of every successful business. However, staying on top of all interactions—whether it's responding to inquiries, following up on leads, or keeping customers informed—can be a time-consuming task, especially for businesses with large client lists. That's where AI-powered bot programs integrated with Customer Relationship Management (CRM) tools like Follow Up Boss can make a significant impact.

In this chapter, we'll explore how you can use bot programs to automate text messaging in your CRM system, ensuring timely follow-ups, personalized communication, and consistent engagement with leads and clients. By leveraging AI bots to handle text communications, you'll save time, improve client satisfaction, and increase the likelihood of closing deals.

## Step 1: Automating Follow-Ups with Text Bots

One of the most time-consuming tasks in client relationship management is following up with leads and clients. Whether it's sending reminders, confirming appointments, or checking in with potential buyers, text messaging is a powerful tool for engaging with clients in real-time. AI-powered bots integrated into your CRM system can automate this entire process:

1. **Automated Lead Follow-Up:** AI bots can automatically send personalized follow-up texts to new leads, ensuring they receive timely responses even when you're unavailable. For example, if a potential client fills out a form or inquires about a property, the bot can send a welcome message with relevant information.
2. **Drip Campaigns via SMS:** For leads that require nurturing over time, text bots can send a series of follow-up messages, keeping them engaged until they are ready to move forward. These automated messages can be tailored based on the lead's behavior or interest, providing them with valuable information, promotions, or reminders.
3. **Appointment Reminders:** If your business involves scheduled appointments or meetings, text bots can automatically send reminders to clients. This reduces the chance of no-shows and ensures that clients stay on top of their commitments.

## Step 2: Personalizing Communication with AI Bots

While automation is key, personalization remains crucial in building strong client relationships. AI bots integrated with CRMs like Follow Up Boss are designed to send messages that feel personal and relevant to each client:

1. **Dynamic Text Customization:** AI bots can dynamically pull customer data, such as names, property preferences, or recent interactions, to customize the content of each message. This ensures that your follow-ups don't feel like generic, automated responses.
2. **Behavior-Based Messaging:** Bots can be programmed to recognize specific behaviors and trigger messages based on actions taken by clients. For example, if a lead opens an email or clicks on a listing link, the bot can follow up with a tailored message, offering more details about the property or asking if they have any questions.

3. **Timing and Frequency Adjustments:** AI bots can be programmed to send messages at optimal times, based on when clients are most likely to engage. Whether it's sending a text during business hours or scheduling messages for evenings or weekends, bots ensure your communication is always timely.

## Step 3: Managing Multiple Conversations Simultaneously

For businesses with a large client base, manually handling text communications can be overwhelming. AI bots integrated with your CRM allow you to manage multiple conversations at once, ensuring no lead is forgotten or neglected:

1. **Simultaneous Conversations:** Bots can simultaneously engage with multiple leads, responding to inquiries, sending follow-ups, and even handling complex questions—without ever dropping the ball. This enables you to scale your communication efforts without hiring additional staff.
2. **Lead Segmentation:** AI bots can segment leads based on their responses or behavior, ensuring that the right messages go to the right people at the right time. For example, leads who express interest in specific property types can receive targeted texts about those properties, while others may receive general market updates.
3. **Escalating to Human Agents:** While bots are powerful for handling routine inquiries and follow-ups, sometimes a human touch is needed. AI bots can identify when a conversation requires human intervention (e.g., complex questions or a customer complaint) and seamlessly transfer the conversation to a sales representative or support team member.

## Step 4: Integrating with Follow Up Boss for Seamless Communication

Follow Up Boss is a powerful CRM tool that helps real estate agents manage leads, automate follow-ups, and track customer interactions. By integrating AI-powered text bots with Follow Up Boss, you can enhance your communication capabilities and automate routine tasks more effectively:

1. **Automated Text Messaging Campaigns:** With Follow Up Boss and AI bots, you can set up automated text campaigns that send messages based on specific lead stages or actions taken by clients. For example, when a lead moves from "New" to "Hot," the bot can trigger a series of text messages to nurture that relationship further.
2. **Tracking and Reporting:** AI bots integrated with Follow Up Boss can track text message performance, providing insights into open rates, responses, and client engagement. This data allows you to adjust your messaging strategies and improve future follow-ups.
3. **Client Database Syncing:** As clients interact with the text bot, the CRM system automatically logs the interactions and updates the client's profile. This ensures that all communication history is available in one place, allowing your team to have a full view of each lead's status and engagement history.

## Step 5: Measuring and Optimizing SMS Campaigns

To ensure that your text message campaigns are effective, it's important to continuously measure their performance and make data-driven adjustments. AI tools integrated with Follow Up Boss can help you optimize your SMS strategies:

1. **Open Rates and Response Tracking:** AI bots can track the effectiveness of text campaigns by monitoring how many clients open and respond to the messages. This data can be used to fine-tune messaging content, timing, and frequency.

2. **A/B Testing:** AI bots can conduct A/B testing on different text message variations to see which phrasing, tone, or call-to-action resonates best with your audience. For example, you can test different offers, links, or headlines to improve conversion rates.
3. **Client Feedback Collection:** Bots can also solicit feedback directly from clients, asking them for their opinions or satisfaction ratings. This feedback can be used to improve communication strategies and adjust the messaging based on client preferences.

## Step 6: Enhancing Client Relationships Through Consistent Communication

The ultimate goal of using AI-powered text bots in your CRM is to build stronger, more consistent relationships with clients. By automating follow-ups and keeping communication seamless, you'll ensure that clients feel valued and stay engaged throughout their journey with your business:

1. **Nurturing Long-Term Relationships:** AI bots can continue to engage with clients even after the initial sale, sending periodic check-ins, updates on new offerings, or helpful tips. This ongoing communication builds trust and keeps your business top-of-mind.
2. **Client Retention:** Automated text communication can help ensure that clients feel connected and informed, which is key to improving retention rates. Happy clients are more likely to refer others or return for future business, driving sustained growth for your company.
3. **Customer Service Availability:** By offering 24/7 automated communication, your clients can receive responses to their inquiries at any time, even when your team is not available. This improves customer satisfaction by ensuring they never feel neglected.

### "Get Real" for Real Estate

For real estate businesses, text messaging is an essential tool for lead management and customer service:

- **Property Inquiries:** When a client expresses interest in a property, an AI bot can instantly send them property details, schedule a viewing, and follow up with a text to answer any questions they may have.
- **Appointment Reminders:** Automated SMS reminders for property showings or meetings ensure that clients don't forget their appointments, improving attendance rates.
- **Lead Nurturing:** AI-powered bots can nurture leads over time by sending them property updates, market news, or personalized messages based on their preferences, keeping them engaged and moving down the sales funnel.

## Wrapping Up

By integrating AI-powered text messaging bots into your CRM system like Follow Up Boss, you can automate follow-ups, engage leads more effectively, and ensure that no client is left behind. With personalized, timely communication, you'll strengthen your client relationships, increase conversions, and streamline your sales process.

# Chapter 12: Using Auto-Clickers for Text Messaging While Avoiding Spam Detection

In the world of digital marketing and customer relationship management (CRM), reaching out to clients and leads through text messages is an effective communication tool. However, with the increase in the use of automated tools, there is also an increasing risk of triggering spam filters or violating messaging platform policies, which could result in your messages being flagged or your number being blocked.

In this chapter, we'll explore how to use auto-clicker tools to send text messages at scale, while maintaining a low risk of triggering spam detection. We'll discuss best practices for using auto-clickers effectively, the limitations you need to be aware of, and strategies to ensure that your messages are seen as legitimate and not flagged as spam.

## Step 1: Understanding Auto-Clickers for SMS Messaging

An auto-clicker is a software tool that automates repetitive tasks by simulating human actions. In the context of text messaging, auto-clickers can be used to send messages through your CRM or messaging platform, mimicking the behavior of manually clicking to send a message.

These tools can be beneficial when you need to send a large number of texts, such as follow-ups, promotional offers, or appointment reminders. By automating the process, you can save time and effort, ensuring that messages are sent efficiently. However, if not used carefully, this can raise red flags with the platform, resulting in spam detection.

## Step 2: Why Spam Detection Is a Concern

Spam filters are designed to protect users from unsolicited or irrelevant messages. Messaging platforms such as Twilio, SendGrid, and other communication services typically monitor and detect suspicious activity, including:

- **Sending too many messages in a short amount of time.**
- **Sending identical or similar messages to multiple recipients.**
- **Using suspicious IP addresses or automated bots that don't behave like human users.**

If you send too many messages in a short period, especially from the same phone number or IP address, it could trigger spam detection algorithms, which might flag or block your account, effectively halting your ability to communicate with clients.

## Step 3: How to Use Auto-Clickers Safely for Text Messaging

While auto-clickers can help you automate the texting process, it's crucial to use them strategically to avoid being flagged for spam. Here are a few key practices to follow:

### 1. Limit the Number of Messages Sent Per Day

The most critical aspect of avoiding spam detection is limiting the volume of messages you send each day. Sending too many messages in a short period is one of the most common triggers for spam detection.

- **Rule of Thumb:** Do not send more than 100 messages per day using auto-clickers. This helps keep your activity within acceptable limits and mimics the behavior of a human sender. Platforms typically expect personal accounts or businesses to send messages at a lower rate, so sending 100 messages per day is generally considered safe.
- **Gradual Increase:** If you are just starting to use auto-clickers, consider starting with a smaller batch (e.g., 20–30 messages per day) and gradually increasing the number over time. This helps your number or account avoid appearing suspicious to spam detection systems.

## 2. Avoid Repetitive or Identical Messages

Sending the same message to multiple recipients without variation can be a red flag for spam detection systems. When using an auto-clicker, vary the content of your messages to make them more personalized and dynamic. Here are a few suggestions:

- **Personalization:** Include the recipient's name, recent interactions, or specific details about the product or service they are interested in. For example, instead of sending the same generic message to all leads, include different property details, personalized offers, or appointment reminders.
- **Randomize Content:** Slightly vary the wording or tone of your messages. For instance, if you're sending reminders about an appointment, you can rotate the way you phrase the message, making each text feel more tailored to the recipient.

## 3. Time Your Messages Properly

Sending a large number of messages all at once is a surefire way to get flagged as spam. To avoid this, you should space out your messages throughout the day, mimicking natural texting behavior. You can achieve this by setting the auto-clicker to send texts at random intervals:

- **Spread the Load:** Use auto-clickers to send messages over several hours, not all at once. For example, instead of sending 100 texts in one hour, spread them out over the course of the day or evening.
- **Use Human-Like Timing:** Mimic the natural behavior of a human user by varying the time intervals between each message. If you send several messages in a row with the same frequency, it may appear suspicious. Instead, space out messages randomly, so it doesn't look like they are being sent by a bot.

## 4. Utilize Different Phone Numbers or IP Addresses

If you need to send a larger volume of messages than what's recommended (100 per day), consider using multiple phone numbers or accounts to distribute the workload. However, be cautious with this approach, as using too many numbers or trying to obscure your identity can appear suspicious.

- **Multiple Numbers:** Using multiple phone numbers can spread out the risk. For example, instead of sending 300 messages from a single number, you can send 100 messages each from three different numbers.
- **Distributed IPs:** If you're using IP-based messaging services, rotate between different IP addresses to prevent your activity from being flagged as bot-like or suspicious.

## 5. Use Captchas and Verification Processes

Many auto-clickers come with built-in Captchas or other verification processes to ensure that the clicks being made are human. These tools can help prevent detection systems from flagging your activity as spam.

- **Captcha Features:** Enable Captcha protection if available. Some auto-clickers can mimic human-like behavior to complete Captchas, reducing the risk of detection.
- **Phone Number Verification:** Some messaging platforms require phone number verification (e.g., through two-factor authentication) to ensure the legitimacy of accounts. Always complete these processes when prompted to ensure your account stays in good standing.

### 6. Monitor and Respond to Client Feedback

Even with the best practices in place, it's important to stay vigilant and monitor how your clients are responding to your messages. If clients report that they're receiving excessive or unwanted texts, it could trigger spam detection or negatively affect your reputation.

- **Respect Opt-Out Requests:** Always provide clients with an option to opt-out of your communications (e.g., "Reply STOP to unsubscribe"). This helps ensure that you're following best practices and reducing the likelihood of your number being flagged.
- **Engage Responsively:** If a client replies to a message, respond promptly and appropriately. This ensures that your conversations maintain a personal touch and don't appear robotic or overly automated.

## Step 4: Monitoring and Analytics

Once you begin using auto-clickers to send texts, it's essential to track the performance and ensure that your messages are being delivered successfully without triggering spam filters:

1. **Monitor Delivery Rates:** Track how many messages are successfully delivered versus how many are blocked or fail to send. If your delivery rate starts dropping, it may indicate that you're being flagged as spam.

2. **Track Response Rates:** Track client responses to your messages. If the response rate is low, or clients are reporting that they're not receiving your messages, it may indicate that your texts are being flagged or blocked.

## Step 5: Legal and Ethical Considerations

When using any automated messaging tool, it's important to remain compliant with laws and regulations, such as the Telephone Consumer Protection Act (TCPA) in the U.S. or the General Data Protection Regulation (GDPR) in the EU. These laws regulate how businesses can contact customers via text and impose strict penalties for violations.

- **Obtain Consent:** Always ensure that you have explicit consent from clients or leads before sending them marketing or promotional text messages.
- **Comply with Unsubscribe Requests:** Respect any requests for clients to opt-out of receiving further messages, and immediately stop sending them texts once they've unsubscribed.

## Wrapping Up

Auto-clickers can be a powerful tool for automating text messaging and streamlining communication with clients and leads. However, to avoid triggering spam detection systems, you must use these tools with caution. By limiting the number of texts sent per day, personalizing content, varying your timing, and monitoring your results, you can effectively use auto-clickers to improve client engagement without risking your business's reputation or your messaging platform's standing.

# Chapter 13: Setting Up Your TikTok Account & Growing Your Presence

**Step 1. Setting Up Your TikTok Account**

Before diving into the world of TikTok, you need to set up your account. Here's a step-by-step guide:

- **Download the App**: Visit the App Store (iOS) or Google Play Store (Android) and download TikTok. Open the app once installed.
- **Sign Up**: You can sign up using your email, phone number, or even your existing social media accounts (Facebook, Google, etc.). If you're using it for business, consider signing up through a business email to keep things professional.
- **Create Your Profile**: Choose a profile picture that represents you or your brand. Make sure it's high quality and easily recognizable. For the username, pick something memorable, simple, and ideally related to your niche.
- **Fill Out Your Bio**: This is your chance to introduce yourself. Keep it short, fun, and specific to your brand or content style. If you're a business, include what you offer or a call-to-action (e.g., "Follow for daily beauty tips!" or "Shop my collection below!").

- **Set Up Privacy**: You can adjust who can view your content, comment, or send you messages. If you're starting out and building an audience, you might want to make your account public so people can discover you.

---

## Getting an Ads Account

Once your TikTok account is ready, you'll want to leverage TikTok's powerful advertising tools to expand your reach. Here's how to set up an ads account:

- **Access TikTok Ads Manager**: Go to TikTok Ads and sign up for an account. You'll need to provide your business name, country, and time zone.
- **Create a Campaign**: Choose your campaign objective (e.g., traffic, conversions, app installs, etc.). TikTok has a variety of ad formats, so pick one that aligns with your goals (e.g., in-feed ads, brand takeovers, or sponsored hashtag challenges).
- **Target Your Audience**: TikTok offers robust targeting options, including demographics, interests, and behaviors. Be specific about who you want to reach to ensure your ads hit the right people.
- **Set Your Budget**: You can choose a daily or total budget for your campaigns. Start small to test which ads work best before scaling up.
- **Launch Your Ads**: Once you've set everything up, launch your ads and monitor their performance in the TikTok Ads Manager. Adjust your targeting, budget, or creatives based on the results.

## Step 2: Understanding TikTok's Ad Formats

TikTok offers several ad formats, each designed to fit into the platform's native, engaging style. Choosing the right ad format depends on your campaign objective and the type of content you want to share:

## 2.1 In-Feed Ads

These are short video ads that appear on users' For You Page (FYP) while they're scrolling through content. They blend seamlessly with organic TikTok content.

- **Length**: Typically between 9-15 seconds.
- **Call-to-Action**: Include a clear CTA, such as "Shop Now," "Learn More," or "Sign Up," to encourage user interaction.
- **Placement**: In-Feed ads are placed within the user's feed, similar to how organic TikTok content appears.

## 2.2 Branded Hashtag Challenges

Branded Hashtag Challenges encourage TikTok users to create content using your branded hashtag. This is a fun and interactive way to boost engagement and generate user-generated content.

- **User Participation**: You create a challenge and encourage users to participate by creating their own videos that feature your product, service, or brand.
- **Goal**: Increase brand awareness and engagement through viral content.
- **Example**: A fitness brand might create a challenge like "#30DaysToFit" and ask users to share their progress.

## 2.3 Top View Ads

Top View ads appear when users first open the TikTok app, guaranteeing maximum visibility. These full-screen, auto-play video ads are great for driving attention and awareness.

- **Length**: Up to 60 seconds.
- **Positioning**: Appears as the first thing a user sees when they open TikTok, so it's excellent for impactful brand launches or promotions.

### 2.4 Branded Effects

Branded Effects allow users to engage with special filters, stickers, and effects designed around your brand. This format encourages user interaction while showcasing your product in a fun, creative way.

- **Goal**: Drive engagement and encourage organic user-created content.
- **Example**: A cosmetics brand might create a filter that shows off their latest makeup products.

# Step 3: Creating Compelling TikTok Ad Content

Creating effective TikTok content is key to capturing the attention of users, especially since TikTok is a fast-paced platform where users scroll through content quickly. Here are some best practices for crafting compelling ads:

### 3.1 Be Authentic and Entertaining

TikTok is known for its fun, lighthearted, and authentic content. Users want to engage with ads that feel real and relatable, not overly polished or sales-y.

- **Show Behind-the-Scenes**: Take your audience behind the scenes of your business. Whether it's showcasing the production process, team, or a "day in the life" at your company, authentic content creates a deeper connection with your audience.
- **Use Humor**: Humor is a great way to capture attention and encourage users to engage with your brand. Whether it's through clever wordplay, lighthearted skits, or fun challenges, humor can go a long way in building brand affinity.

### 3.2 Keep it Short and Sweet

TikTok users are accustomed to quick, snackable content. While ads can be up to 60 seconds long, it's often best to keep your message concise and punchy, especially for In-Feed Ads.

- **Hook Your Audience in the First Few Seconds**: The first 3 seconds of your video are critical for capturing attention. Start with an eye-catching visual or bold statement to draw viewers in.
- **Clear Call-to-Action (CTA)**: Make sure your ad includes a clear CTA that tells the viewer what to do next. This could be to visit your website, shop your collection, or follow your TikTok page.

### 3.3 Use Music and Trends

TikTok is driven by music and viral trends. Incorporating trending songs or challenges into your ads can increase the chances of your content being discovered.

- **Leverage Popular Songs**: Use music that is trending on the platform, as this helps your content blend into the feed and increases the likelihood of engagement.
- **Participate in Trends**: Keep an eye on popular trends and challenges that align with your brand. Participating in trends can help your brand feel more connected to the TikTok community.

## Step 4: The Rules of Engagement on TikTok

While TikTok's algorithm prioritizes organic engagement, it's important to understand the rules of engagement for advertisers to ensure your content is seen and appreciated by your target audience.

### 4.1 Stay Compliant with TikTok's Advertising Guidelines

TikTok has specific advertising guidelines that you must follow to ensure that your content is approved and doesn't violate community standards. Here are a few key points to keep in mind:

- **Prohibited Content**: TikTok prohibits ads that contain deceptive content, harmful behaviors, or misleading claims. Avoid making exaggerated claims or promoting harmful products.
- **Targeting Rules**: TikTok requires advertisers to ensure that their targeting practices align with privacy laws. Make sure you are not violating any regulations, such as GDPR or CCPA, when collecting user data or personal information.
- **Sensitive Content**: If your ad includes content that could be considered sensitive (e.g., political messaging, alcohol, gambling, or adult content), make sure you're following TikTok's specific policies for those industries.

## 4.2 Engage with Your Audience

Engagement on TikTok goes beyond simply creating ads—it's about building a community. Respond to comments, join trending conversations, and interact with your followers to boost your visibility and increase brand loyalty.

- **Respond to Comments**: Take the time to reply to comments and engage with your audience. Whether it's answering questions or thanking users for their support, engagement is key to building relationships.
- **Collaborate with Influencers**: TikTok influencers have a massive following and can help amplify your message. Partnering with influencers who align with your brand values can help extend your reach and add authenticity to your campaign.

## 4.3 Be Consistent with Posting

TikTok rewards consistency. To build a loyal following and keep your audience engaged, it's important to post regularly.

- **Post Frequently**: Aim to post at least once a day, but don't sacrifice quality for quantity. Consistency in posting helps build momentum and increases the chances of your content being featured on the For You Page (FYP).

- **Use Hashtags Effectively**: Hashtags are vital for discovery on TikTok. Use trending hashtags or create a branded hashtag to make it easier for users to find your content.

## Get Real: TikTok for Real Estate

As a real estate professional, TikTok may seem like an unconventional platform for promoting your listings or services, but it can be a goldmine for reaching potential clients, especially younger homebuyers or renters. In this section, we'll break down how you can apply the tips from the TikTok advertising chapter to your real estate business. Let's dive into how to make TikTok work for you, from setting up ads to engaging with your audience.

### 1. Setting Up Your TikTok Ads Account for Real Estate

First things first—set up your TikTok Ads account just as we discussed. However, with real estate, your campaign objectives may differ from other businesses. Your focus might be on:

- **Lead generation**: Encouraging potential buyers to schedule a showing or download a property brochure.
- **Brand awareness**: Building your presence as the go-to local expert in your real estate market.
- **Traffic**: Driving people to your website or specific property listings.

Choose the appropriate objective for your goal. If you're promoting a property, a **traffic** campaign that links directly to the listing page might be best. If you're focusing on building your reputation in the area, **brand awareness** or **video views** campaigns would work better.

### 2. Content Creation for Real Estate Listings

When creating your ads, think of TikTok as a storytelling platform rather than just an advertising space. Here's how you can apply the content tips specifically for real estate:

- **Give a Tour of Properties**: A great way to showcase properties is by giving short virtual tours. Highlight key features of the property with music and text overlays. For example, showcase a living room's spaciousness with a catchy song, then add text that says "Imagine yourself here" to evoke emotion.
- **Before-and-After Transformations**: Post videos showing the transformation of a property you've renovated. Use trending sounds or viral challenges to make the content feel more fun and engaging.
- **Client Testimonials**: Share real customer testimonials on how you helped them find their dream home. Clients sharing their stories humanizes your brand and builds trust.
- **Neighborhood Spotlights**: Highlight local businesses or popular spots in your area. Showcase your knowledge of the community by posting a video of a favorite coffee shop or park nearby your listings.

## Wrapping Up

TikTok offers a powerful platform for businesses to advertise and connect with a massive audience. By setting up your ads account, choosing the right ad format, creating authentic and engaging content, and following TikTok's rules of engagement, you can effectively leverage this platform to drive brand awareness, increase sales, and build lasting customer relationships.

In the next chapter, we'll dive into advanced strategies for using TikTok's analytics to track ad performance and optimize future campaigns for maximum results.

# Chapter 14: Analyzing Your TikTok Ad Performance: Using Analytics to Optimize Your Strategy

In this chapter, we'll dive into TikTok's analytics tools and how you can use the data to measure the performance of your ads, optimize your strategy, and ensure your content is delivering the best possible results. Understanding the metrics behind your TikTok campaigns is key to improving future content, targeting the right audience, and maximizing your return on investment (ROI). Whether you're running ads for a real estate business, an e-commerce store, or a service-based company, data-driven decisions are critical to scaling your efforts.

## Step 1: Understanding TikTok Analytics

TikTok offers robust analytics tools through its Ads Manager platform, which provides detailed insights into how your campaigns are performing. By using these insights, you can refine your strategy and optimize your content to meet your business goals. Here's how to navigate TikTok's analytics dashboard:

### 1.1 Accessing Your TikTok Analytics

To access TikTok Analytics, follow these steps:

1. **Log into Your Ads Manager Account**: Head over to the TikTok Ads Manager dashboard.
2. **Campaigns Overview**: Click on the "Campaign" tab, where you can view a summary of your active, paused, and completed campaigns.
3. **Ad Group and Ads Performance**: Click on individual campaigns to drill down into specific ad groups and individual ads. Here, you'll be able to analyze each ad's performance.

## 1.2 Key Metrics to Monitor

TikTok provides a wide range of data points to track the effectiveness of your campaigns. The most important metrics to focus on include:

- **Impressions**: The number of times your ad was displayed to users. While this doesn't reflect engagement, it gives you an idea of how many people saw your content.
- **Click-Through Rate (CTR)**: The percentage of viewers who clicked on your ad after seeing it. A higher CTR generally indicates that your ad is compelling and relevant.
- **Conversion Rate**: The percentage of clicks that led to a specific action (such as a form submission or purchase). This is crucial for measuring how well your ad drives meaningful results.
- **Cost Per Click (CPC)**: The average cost you pay for each click on your ad. Lower CPC can indicate efficient targeting and ad design.
- **Cost Per Conversion (CPCV)**: The average cost of acquiring a conversion, such as a lead or sale. This metric is essential to track your ROI.
- **Engagement Rate**: This includes likes, comments, shares, and saves. High engagement rates typically mean your content resonates with your audience.

- **View Through Rate (VTR)**: The percentage of viewers who watched your ad to completion. High VTR indicates that your ad is engaging and holds the viewer's attention.

## Step 2: Interpreting Your Data and Making Adjustments

Once you've familiarized yourself with the key metrics, it's time to analyze the data and make adjustments to improve your future campaigns.

### 2.1 Analyzing Audience Behavior

TikTok's analytics also provides insights into who's engaging with your content. For businesses, understanding your audience's demographics can help you target your ads more effectively. Look at:

- **Age and Gender**: Are you reaching the right demographic for your business? For example, if you're in real estate, you may want to target individuals aged 25-45 who are likely to be in the market for their first home.
- **Geographic Location**: TikTok allows you to track where your audience is located. This is especially useful for businesses with a local or regional focus.
- **Interests**: Understanding what topics your audience is interested in can help you refine your targeting and content. For example, if your real estate videos perform better with users interested in home décor, consider incorporating home styling tips into future videos.

### 2.2 Evaluating Ad Formats

If you've tested multiple ad formats (In-Feed, Branded Hashtag Challenges, etc.), it's important to assess which ones are performing best. For example:

- **In-Feed Ads** might drive more website traffic, but **Branded Hashtag Challenges** could generate higher engagement rates and user-generated content.
- **Top View Ads** could be great for building brand awareness, but might not always convert as well as In-Feed or Click-to-Website ads for direct sales.

Look at which format yields the highest ROI for your goals and budget, and adjust your strategy accordingly.

### 2.3 Experimenting with A/B Testing

A/B testing is crucial for refining your TikTok ad strategy. Test different variations of your ads to see which ones perform best. Here are a few elements to experiment with:

- **Video Length**: Does a 15-second video generate better results than a 60-second one? Try both and compare their performance.
- **Ad Copy**: Try variations in your headlines or captions. For example, compare a headline that emphasizes "luxury living" versus "affordable homes" and see which resonates more with your audience.
- **Call-to-Action (CTA)**: Try different CTAs like "Buy Now," "Learn More," or "Book a Tour." Measure which CTA drives more conversions.
- **Targeting**: Experiment with different audience segments. For instance, if you're targeting young professionals for real estate, try narrowing your audience by occupation (e.g., tech workers or teachers).

Use the results to tweak your future campaigns and fine-tune your ad content.

## Step 3: Optimizing Your TikTok Ads for Better Results

Based on the insights from TikTok's analytics, you can begin optimizing your campaigns. Here's how:

### 3.1 Refining Your Target Audience

If your data shows that a specific demographic is engaging with your content more than others, consider refining your targeting to focus on that group. For example:

- If you're selling real estate and notice that people aged 30-45 are more likely to convert, adjust your targeting to prioritize this age group.
- If your ad is getting a lot of engagement from users in specific locations, narrow your targeting to those areas.

### 3.2 Adjusting Bidding and Budget

If you're getting a lot of clicks but not enough conversions, it could be a sign that your ad targeting or landing page isn't fully optimized. On the flip side, if you're getting good conversions but your budget is too small, increasing your daily ad spend can help you scale your success.

- **Increase budget for high-performing campaigns**: If you have a campaign with a high CTR and a low CPC, increasing your budget can help reach more people without significantly increasing costs.
- **Adjust bid strategies**: If your campaign has a low CTR or conversion rate, consider adjusting your bid strategy. For example, if you're using the automatic bid option, try switching to a manual bid to have more control over your costs.

### 3.3 Improving Creative Content

If your ads aren't performing well, it could be time to revise your creative content. Based on the engagement and view-through rates, consider:

- **Improving video quality**: Ensure your videos are visually engaging and professionally shot. Poor production quality can hurt engagement.
- **Refining the message**: Make sure your message aligns with the audience's expectations. If you're selling

real estate, focus on showcasing the best aspects of a property or neighborhood, and avoid excessive jargon.
- **Using music and trends**: Incorporating popular songs or viral trends into your content can increase engagement and visibility. Pay attention to which trends are popular in your target audience and try to incorporate them into your content.

## Step 4: Measuring Long-Term Success

To gauge long-term success, you need to look beyond the immediate results of your ad campaigns. Here's how to track sustained growth:

- **Track Lead Generation**: If you're collecting leads through your TikTok ads (e.g., email sign-ups, consultation bookings, etc.), track how these leads convert over time. Use your CRM or marketing automation tools to measure the effectiveness of TikTok leads in the sales funnel.
- **Build Brand Loyalty**: Look at repeat engagement from the same users. If people are consistently liking, commenting, or sharing your content, you are building a loyal audience.
- **Monitor Lifetime Value (LTV)**: If you're running sales or lead generation campaigns, track how much each customer brings in over time. This will help you understand the true ROI of your TikTok ads.

## Wrapping Up

TikTok analytics is a powerful tool for refining your advertising strategy and optimizing content. By regularly reviewing your data, making adjustments to your campaigns, and improving your creative, you can enhance your TikTok ad performance, maximize your ROI, and build a loyal, engaged audience. Remember that analytics is an ongoing process—constantly tweak and test your ads to ensure your strategies are evolving with your business goals.

In the next chapter, we'll explore how to use AI-powered tools to further enhance your TikTok marketing efforts and help you automate the process of optimizing campaigns.

# Chapter 15: Supercharging Your TikTok Marketing with AI-Powered Tools

In this chapter, we'll explore how AI-powered tools can take your TikTok marketing efforts to the next level by automating tasks, improving ad performance, and optimizing campaigns. With AI, you can gain deeper insights, fine-tune your content, and save time while scaling your advertising efforts. Whether you're running a single campaign or managing multiple TikTok accounts, these tools can help streamline your workflow and enhance your results.

## Step 1: Leveraging AI for Content Creation

One of the most labor-intensive aspects of TikTok marketing is creating fresh, engaging content. AI-powered tools can help automate content generation, optimize visuals, and assist with video editing, allowing you to focus on strategy and engagement.

### 1.1 AI Video Editing Tools

There are several AI-powered video editing tools that can help you streamline the process of creating TikTok content. These tools can automatically trim and enhance your footage, add special effects, and even suggest video formats based on trends. Some popular AI video editing tools include:

- **Magisto**: This tool uses AI to automatically edit your videos by selecting the best clips, adding effects, and even suggesting music based on your content type.
- **InVideo**: InVideo allows you to create professional-looking TikTok videos quickly. It comes with pre-built templates and AI-powered suggestions for adding text overlays, transitions, and visual effects to your videos.
- **Pictory**: With Pictory, you can convert long-form videos into bite-sized TikTok clips by selecting key moments and adding engaging captions and subtitles—all powered by AI.

Using AI video editing tools, you can create high-quality, on-brand content in a fraction of the time it would take manually, while keeping up with TikTok's fast-paced content trends.

### 1.2 AI-Generated Music and Sounds

Music is key to TikTok's success, and AI can help you find the perfect soundtrack for your videos. AI-powered music generators, like **Aiva** and **Amper Music**, can create custom music based on your preferences, mood, or video content. This is especially helpful for real estate professionals who want a unique, branded sound to accompany their property tours or virtual walkthroughs.

By using AI-generated music, you can ensure your content stands out from the crowd while maintaining a cohesive brand experience.

## Step 2: Automating TikTok Ad Management

AI tools can also automate and optimize your TikTok ad campaigns, allowing you to focus on strategy rather than manual adjustments. Here's how:

### 2.1 Automated Bid and Budget Management

AI-driven platforms, like **AdEspresso** and **WordStream**, offer automated bidding and budget optimization features for TikTok ads. These tools use machine learning algorithms to analyze your ad performance in real-time and automatically adjust your bids and budget allocation to maximize ROI.

For example, if a particular ad set is performing well, these platforms can increase its budget while reducing the spend on underperforming ads. This helps ensure you're always putting your money where it matters most.

### 2.2 Audience Targeting Optimization

AI-powered tools can help you reach your ideal audience by continuously refining your targeting. Platforms like **Optmyzr** and **Adzooma** use machine learning to analyze your ad data and recommend more accurate audience segments based on behaviors, interests, demographics, and even psychographics.

These tools can also create lookalike audiences—people who share similar characteristics to your current customers—ensuring you're targeting users who are more likely to engage with your content or make a purchase.

## Step 3: AI-Driven Analytics for Performance Optimization

AI-powered analytics tools can help you track and interpret key metrics in real-time, providing you with deeper insights into how your TikTok campaigns are performing. These tools take the guesswork out of analyzing your data, helping you make more informed decisions.

### 3.1 AI-Powered Insights with TikTok Analytics

TikTok's native analytics is a great starting point, but AI tools can provide an even more in-depth look at your campaigns. Tools like **Sprout Social** and **SocialBee** integrate with TikTok and use AI to offer advanced analytics, such as:

- **Sentiment Analysis**: These tools can gauge the mood and sentiment of comments, mentions, and engagements, helping you understand how people feel about your content and brand.
- **Performance Forecasting**: AI can predict the future performance of your ads based on historical data, allowing you to optimize your strategy proactively.
- **Audience Segmentation**: AI can analyze engagement trends and identify new audience segments, allowing you to fine-tune your content and targeting to maximize conversions.

By using AI to dive deeper into your performance data, you can make faster adjustments and continuously improve your TikTok marketing strategy.

### 3.2 AI for Trend Analysis

Keeping up with TikTok trends can be challenging, but AI-powered trend analysis tools like **TrendTok** or **Trends.co** can help. These tools analyze TikTok's vast pool of content and identify emerging trends, popular sounds, hashtags, and video formats. By tapping into these insights, you can create timely, on-trend content that's more likely to go viral and engage your audience.

AI tools can also suggest specific trends to leverage based on your niche, whether it's real estate, fashion, or food. For instance, if a trend related to home decor is gaining traction, you can quickly create content that capitalizes on it, positioning yourself as an expert in the field.

## Step 4: AI Chatbots for Lead Generation and Customer Engagement

An often-overlooked feature of AI is the ability to automate customer interactions through chatbots. These bots can answer questions, collect information, and even qualify leads without any human intervention. For TikTok marketers, AI chatbots can be integrated into your landing pages or TikTok bio link to handle inquiries and lead generation.

- **ManyChat**: ManyChat is a chatbot platform that integrates with TikTok and helps businesses engage with leads by sending automated messages and follow-ups. If someone expresses interest in your real estate listings, the chatbot can collect their contact information, schedule a call, or provide more details about a property.
- **Tidio**: Tidio offers an AI-powered chatbot that can engage with your TikTok audience in real-time. It can also integrate with CRM systems, allowing you to follow up with leads immediately, providing a seamless experience for potential clients.

## Step 5: Using AI for Content Scheduling and Posting

AI tools can help you plan, schedule, and post content at the optimal times for engagement. Platforms like **Hootsuite**, **Buffer**, and **Lately** offer AI-driven scheduling and content management features that can automatically post your TikTok videos based on the time of day when your audience is most active.

These tools analyze engagement data and recommend the best times to post, which can help increase visibility and interaction. Some platforms even suggest relevant hashtags and captions based on your content, saving you time and ensuring your posts are optimized for reach.

## Wrapping Up

AI-powered tools are essential for maximizing the effectiveness of your TikTok marketing efforts. From automating content creation and video editing to optimizing ad targeting and audience engagement, AI can save you time, enhance your campaigns, and improve your overall marketing ROI. By using these tools, you can stay ahead of trends, make data-driven decisions, and scale your TikTok marketing strategy with ease.

# Chapter 16: Setting Up and Using Instagram, Facebook, and X (formerly Twitter) for Business

In this chapter, we'll guide you through setting up and managing accounts on three of the most popular social media platforms for business: Instagram, Facebook, and X (formerly known as Twitter). Each platform offers unique features and opportunities to engage with your audience, build your brand, and drive sales or leads. Whether you're just getting started or looking to refine your social media strategy, this chapter will provide the essential steps to leverage these platforms effectively.

## Step 1: Setting Up Your Instagram Business Account

Instagram is a visually-driven platform, perfect for businesses in industries such as fashion, beauty, real estate, and more. Here's how to set up and optimize your Instagram account:

### 1.1 Creating Your Instagram Business Profile

1. **Download the Instagram App**: If you haven't already, download Instagram from the App Store (for iPhone) or Google Play Store (for Android).
2. **Sign Up**: Open the app and sign up with your business email address. Alternatively, you can use a Facebook account to log in.
3. **Switch to a Business Profile**:
   - Go to your profile and tap the three horizontal lines in the top-right corner.
   - Tap **Settings** > **Account** > **Switch to Professional Account**.
   - Choose the **Business** option and select the category that best fits your business.
4. **Complete Your Profile**:
   - **Profile Picture**: Choose a logo or a recognizable image that represents your brand.
   - **Bio**: Write a clear and concise description of your business (e.g., "Your go-to source for home décor inspiration").
   - **Contact Information**: Include your business email, phone number, and physical address if applicable.

## 1.2 Optimizing Your Instagram for Engagement

- **Create a Content Strategy**: Focus on high-quality images, videos, and stories that align with your brand identity. Share behind-the-scenes content, product highlights, customer testimonials, and more.
- **Use Instagram's Features**: Take advantage of features like Stories, Reels, and IGTV to increase engagement and reach. Reels, in particular, can help your business go viral and reach a broader audience.
- **Hashtags**: Research and use relevant hashtags to expand your reach. Include a mix of popular, niche, and branded hashtags in each post.
- **Engage with Followers**: Respond to comments, like and share posts, and engage with other accounts in your industry to build relationships and boost your visibility.

### 1.3 Running Instagram Ads

Instagram ads are managed through Facebook's Ads Manager, which allows you to create a variety of ad formats such as photo, video, carousel, and stories ads. Here's how to set up your first ad:

1. **Link Your Facebook Page**: If you haven't already, connect your Instagram account to your Facebook business page.
2. **Create an Ad**: Go to Facebook Ads Manager and select **Create**. Choose your campaign objective (e.g., website traffic, conversions, brand awareness).
3. **Target Your Audience**: Use Facebook's detailed targeting options to define your audience based on demographics, interests, behaviors, and more.
4. **Set Your Budget and Schedule**: Decide how much you want to spend and set your campaign schedule.
5. **Design Your Ad**: Choose your format, upload creative (images, videos), and write compelling ad copy.
6. **Launch Your Campaign**: Once you're happy with your ad, click **Publish** to launch your campaign.

## Step 2: Setting Up Your Facebook Business Page

Facebook remains one of the most powerful tools for business marketing. With over 2.9 billion monthly active users, it's an essential platform for building brand awareness and connecting with customers. Here's how to set up your Facebook Business Page:

### 2.1 Creating Your Facebook Business Page

1. **Log In to Facebook**: Use your personal Facebook account to create a business page.
2. **Create a Page**:
   - On the left sidebar, click **Pages** > **Create New Page**.

- Choose a page name and category (e.g., "Real Estate Agency" or "Online Boutique").
- Fill out the details, including the business description and contact information.

3. **Upload Your Profile and Cover Photos**: Use high-quality images that reflect your brand.
4. **Complete Your Page**:
   - Add additional information such as location, hours of operation, services, and pricing.
   - Set up a **Call to Action (CTA)** button (e.g., "Contact Us," "Shop Now," or "Book an Appointment").

## 2.2 Building Your Facebook Strategy

- **Post Regularly**: Share a mix of content that educates, entertains, and informs your audience. Include posts about promotions, product launches, customer testimonials, and industry news.
- **Use Facebook Groups**: Join or create groups related to your industry to engage with a targeted audience. It's a great way to build a community and establish your authority.
- **Utilize Facebook Insights**: Monitor your page's performance with Facebook Insights. Track key metrics like reach, engagement, and page views to see what's working.
- **Facebook Ads**: Like Instagram, Facebook Ads are managed through Facebook's Ads Manager. Use the same process to create targeted ad campaigns designed to meet your business goals.

## 2.3 Engaging with Your Audience

- **Respond to Messages**: Use the Facebook Messenger app to connect directly with customers and answer questions quickly.
- **Comments and Reviews**: Regularly check your page for new comments and reviews. Respond to both

positive and negative feedback professionally to maintain a positive reputation.

- **Facebook Live**: Host live streaming events to engage with your audience in real time. You can host Q&A sessions, product demos, or even behind-the-scenes tours.

## Step 3: Setting Up Your X (Formerly Twitter) Account

X is a fast-paced, text-based platform known for short updates and trending topics. It's a great way to share quick announcements, industry news, and engage with your followers in real time.

### 3.1 Creating Your X Account

1. **Sign Up for X**: Go to X.com and sign up with your business email address. You can also sign up with an existing Google or Apple account.
2. **Profile Setup**:
   - **Profile Picture**: Use a clear and recognizable logo or image.
   - **Bio**: Write a concise, 160-character description of your business. Include relevant keywords and a link to your website or landing page.
   - **Cover Photo**: Add a banner image that represents your brand, such as your product line, store, or event.
3. **Verify Your Account**: To increase credibility, apply for a verification badge through X's verification process.

### 3.2 Optimizing Your X for Engagement

- **Tweet Regularly**: Post short, engaging updates regularly. Tweets should be concise, informative, and aligned with your business objectives.
- **Use Hashtags**: Leverage trending and niche hashtags to make your content discoverable.

- **Engage in Real-Time Conversations**: Join in on trending topics and participate in relevant conversations by replying to other tweets and using hashtags.
- **Follow Industry Leaders**: Stay informed about industry news and insights by following influencers, brands, and thought leaders in your space.

### 3.3 Running Ads on X

1. **Access X Ads Manager**: Go to the **X Ads** platform and select **Create Campaign**.
2. **Select Your Campaign Objective**: Choose from options like brand awareness, website clicks, or engagement.
3. **Define Your Audience**: Use X's targeting options to specify demographics, location, interests, and more.
4. **Design Your Ad**: Choose between text, image, or video ads to create compelling content.
5. **Set Your Budget**: Determine how much you're willing to spend per day or on a total campaign basis.
6. **Launch**: Review and launch your ad campaign once everything is set.

### 3.4 Engaging with Your Audience

- **Respond to Tweets**: Monitor mentions of your business and respond promptly to engage with your audience.
- **Run Polls**: Use Twitter polls to gather feedback, ask questions, or engage your followers in fun and interactive ways.
- **Share Visual Content**: Include images and videos in your tweets to improve engagement and visibility.

## Wrapping Up

By setting up and optimizing your Instagram, Facebook, and X (formerly Twitter) accounts, you can build a strong, cohesive social media presence for your business. Each platform offers unique features that can help you connect with your audience, build brand loyalty, and drive sales. Whether you're using

Instagram for visually stunning content, Facebook for community engagement, or X for quick updates, these platforms are essential for modern business marketing.

In the next chapter, we'll explore how to integrate all your social media platforms into a cohesive strategy, helping you streamline your social media marketing and maximize your reach.

# Chapter 17: Integrating Your Social Media Platforms into a Cohesive Strategy

In this chapter, we'll explore how to unify your Instagram, Facebook, and X (formerly Twitter) accounts into a streamlined social media strategy that maximizes your reach, enhances engagement, and ensures consistency across all platforms. By integrating your social media efforts, you can save time, increase brand visibility, and make sure your audience receives a clear, cohesive message no matter where they encounter your business online.

## Step 1: Define Your Social Media Goals

Before diving into integration, it's essential to clearly define your social media goals. Your strategy should align with your overall business objectives. Here are some common social media goals that can guide your approach:

- **Brand Awareness**: Increase visibility and reach by posting consistently and engaging with your audience.
- **Lead Generation**: Use social media to gather leads for sales or email campaigns, offering promotions or value-based content to attract potential clients.
- **Customer Engagement**: Foster strong relationships with your audience by responding to comments, messages, and mentions in real-time.

- **Conversions**: Convert followers into customers by directing them to your website or specific product pages through targeted calls to action.

Once your goals are defined, you can tailor your content, posting schedule, and strategy to meet these objectives across all platforms.

# Step 2: Develop a Consistent Brand Voice and Messaging

Consistency is key when integrating your social media platforms. Your audience should recognize your business across all channels, no matter the platform. To ensure this, you'll need to develop a cohesive brand voice, tone, and messaging that reflects your business values and resonates with your audience.

### 2.1 Define Your Brand Voice

Your brand voice should remain consistent across Instagram, Facebook, and X. Whether you're writing captions, replying to comments, or creating ads, your tone should align with your brand identity. For example:

- **Friendly & Approachable**: Perfect for businesses in the hospitality, lifestyle, or wellness industries.
- **Professional & Authoritative**: Ideal for businesses in finance, consulting, or real estate.
- **Fun & Playful**: Suitable for brands in entertainment, fashion, or food.

Your brand voice should be applied consistently to all your posts, ads, and engagements, whether it's a casual tweet on X, a polished post on Facebook, or an inspirational story on Instagram.

### 2.2 Consistent Visual Identity

Your visual identity should also remain consistent across all platforms. This includes:

- **Profile Pictures & Cover Images**: Use your logo as your profile picture, and make sure your cover photos are relevant to your current marketing campaigns or branding efforts.
- **Color Palette**: Choose a color scheme that reflects your brand and use it consistently in your graphics, posts, and advertisements.
- **Fonts and Design Style**: Pick one or two fonts that represent your business and stick with them for all written content across social media.
- **Image Quality & Style**: Maintain high-quality, visually appealing content that aligns with your brand aesthetics. On Instagram, for example, your feed should reflect your brand's style, while on Facebook, your posts can include a mix of photos, videos, and other types of media.

## Step 3: Create a Unified Content Calendar

To ensure consistent posting and content management across Instagram, Facebook, and X, creating a unified content calendar is crucial. A content calendar will help you plan and organize posts for all platforms while ensuring they align with your overall marketing campaigns.

### 3.1 Choosing Content Types for Each Platform

Each platform has its strengths, and your content should be adapted to fit those strengths:

- **Instagram**: Visual-based content is key. Use high-quality images, videos, Reels, and Stories to showcase your products, services, or behind-the-scenes content. You can also leverage Instagram's interactive features like polls and quizzes to engage your audience.
- **Facebook**: Mix your content to include photos, videos, live streams, articles, and even user-generated content.

Facebook is also ideal for building communities, so share posts that encourage conversation and discussions within your Facebook Groups.

- **X**: Focus on short, text-based content with images or videos. X is perfect for sharing quick updates, news, and engaging in real-time conversations around trending topics.

You should align your content on all three platforms around the same themes, but tailor the formats and delivery to fit the specific platform.

### 3.2 Scheduling and Posting

Using a scheduling tool like **Buffer**, **Hootsuite**, or **Later**, you can automate and manage posts across all platforms. This saves time and ensures consistency in your posting frequency and timing.

Here's how to schedule and post effectively:

1. **Determine Posting Frequency**: Decide how often you want to post on each platform. For example, aim for daily posts on Instagram, 3-4 weekly posts on Facebook, and multiple tweets on X throughout the day.
2. **Set Optimal Posting Times**: Use platform analytics to determine when your audience is most active, and schedule posts during peak engagement times.
3. **Repurpose Content**: Repurpose the same content across platforms, adjusting it to fit the specific requirements. For instance, a long Facebook post can be turned into a short tweet for X, and the images can be shared as part of an Instagram carousel.

## Step 4: Cross-Promote Your Accounts

Cross-promotion is an effective way to drive traffic and engagement between your social media platforms. Here's how to do it:

1.  **Share Instagram Content on Facebook and X**: Share your Instagram posts and Stories on Facebook, and create Twitter threads linking to Instagram content. You can also encourage your X followers to follow you on Instagram for more visual content or updates.
2.  **Direct Traffic Between Platforms**: In your Instagram bio or Facebook posts, include calls to action directing followers to your X account for quick updates or exclusive promotions. On X, you can link to your Instagram page for more detailed content or behind-the-scenes looks.
3.  **Host Contests or Giveaways Across Platforms**: Run a contest or giveaway that requires people to follow you on multiple platforms. For example, "Follow us on Instagram and X for a chance to win!" This increases your reach and drives traffic across your channels.

## Step 5: Analyze and Optimize Performance

To ensure that your integrated social media strategy is successful, it's essential to monitor your performance and adjust accordingly. Use the built-in analytics tools on each platform (Instagram Insights, Facebook Analytics, and X Analytics) to track key metrics like:

- **Engagement**: How many likes, comments, and shares your posts are receiving.
- **Reach and Impressions**: The number of people who see your content.
- **Click-Through Rate (CTR)**: How often people click on links in your posts.
- **Follower Growth**: How many new followers you're gaining over time.

Analyzing this data will help you understand what content works best on each platform and enable you to optimize your strategy for greater engagement and success.

## Wrapping Up

Integrating your Instagram, Facebook, and X accounts into a unified strategy will help streamline your social media marketing efforts, saving time and ensuring that your message is consistent across all channels. By defining your goals, creating a consistent brand voice, scheduling posts, and analyzing performance, you can maximize your reach, engage with your audience, and grow your business online.

In the next chapter, we'll explore how to combine social media efforts with email marketing, CRM tools, and other digital marketing strategies to create a seamless customer experience and increase your conversions.

# Chapter 18: Combining Social Media, Email Marketing, and CRM Tools for a Seamless Customer Experience

In this chapter, we'll dive into the powerful synergy created when you combine your social media efforts with email marketing, CRM tools, and other digital marketing strategies. This integrated approach allows you to create a seamless customer experience, nurture leads effectively, and increase your conversions. By connecting the dots between your various marketing channels, you can deliver targeted content to the right people at the right time, ultimately driving more engagement, sales, and long-term customer loyalty.

## Step 1: Connecting Your Social Media with Email Marketing

Email marketing and social media are two of the most effective channels for engaging with your audience. Combining them can create a powerful customer journey that moves prospects from awareness to conversion.

### 1.1 Collect Leads from Social Media

Start by using your social media platforms to gather leads that you can nurture through email campaigns. Here's how:

- **Lead Magnets**: Offer free resources (e.g., eBooks, checklists, or webinars) on your social media profiles in exchange for email sign-ups. Promote these lead magnets in your posts, Stories, or ads on platforms like Instagram, Facebook, and X.
- **Call-to-Action (CTA)**: Use strong CTAs in your social media posts and bios that encourage followers to join your email list. For example, "Sign up for exclusive offers via our email list" or "Get the latest updates straight to your inbox."
- **Landing Pages**: Create dedicated landing pages on your website where visitors from social media can opt into your email list. You can drive traffic to these pages with Instagram and Facebook Ads or via links in your posts on X.

## 1.2 Sync Social Media Campaigns with Email Campaigns

Once you have a growing email list, synchronize your social media campaigns with email marketing to ensure your messages are consistent and complementary.

- **Cross-Promotion**: Promote your email campaigns on your social media accounts. For instance, let your Instagram followers know that they'll be getting an exclusive offer in your upcoming newsletter.
- **Social Proof**: Use testimonials, user-generated content, or success stories from your social media followers in your emails. This helps to reinforce credibility and trust.
- **Email Content**: Direct your email recipients to your social media profiles by including links to your latest posts or campaigns. Conversely, you can drive social media followers to sign up for your email newsletter for even more value.
- **Personalized Content**: Use information gathered from social media engagement (such as demographics and

behavior) to personalize email content and offers. Tailor email subject lines, copy, and product recommendations to the interests of your subscribers.

## Step 2: Integrating CRM Tools to Manage Customer Data

CRM tools are essential for managing relationships with your customers and streamlining communication. Integrating CRM tools with your social media and email marketing systems enables you to leverage customer data more effectively and create a seamless experience across all touchpoints.

### 2.1 Choose the Right CRM for Your Business

Select a CRM tool that integrates well with your social media platforms and email marketing software. Some popular CRMs include:

- **HubSpot**: Integrates seamlessly with Instagram, Facebook, X, and email platforms like Mailchimp. HubSpot offers robust marketing automation features, allowing you to track customer interactions and segment audiences based on their behavior.
- **Salesforce**: A powerful CRM for larger businesses with advanced features for tracking social media interactions, automating workflows, and nurturing leads.
- **Zoho CRM**: A more affordable option that integrates with social media and email tools, helping you manage and segment customer data.
- **Pipedrive**: A user-friendly CRM that integrates with social media and email marketing tools to track interactions and sales progress.

### 2.2 Use CRM Data to Segment Your Audience

A CRM allows you to segment your audience based on key data points such as:

- **Demographics**: Age, location, and interests can help you personalize both email and social media content.
- **Customer Behavior**: Track how customers interact with your social media and email campaigns. Use this data to send tailored follow-ups or promotions based on engagement levels.
- **Purchase History**: Segment customers who have already made a purchase or shown interest in specific products. You can send them personalized offers or recommendations through both social media ads and email.

### 2.3 Automate Customer Interactions

Automation is one of the biggest advantages of integrating CRM tools with social media and email marketing. By setting up automated workflows, you can ensure that your leads and customers receive the right messages at the right time without manual intervention.

- **Welcome Emails**: Send automated welcome emails when someone subscribes to your email list via social media. Use a friendly tone and provide value (such as an exclusive discount or helpful guide).
- **Abandoned Cart Emails**: If you're running an e-commerce business, you can automate emails to remind customers about abandoned carts. Pair this with targeted ads on social media to bring them back to your website.
- **Follow-Up Sequences**: Based on a customer's activity (such as a recent purchase or social media interaction), set up follow-up email sequences that guide them through the next steps in their customer journey.

# Step 3: Creating a Seamless Customer Experience

The goal of combining social media, email marketing, and CRM tools is to create a seamless customer experience where all interactions feel cohesive and personalized.

## 3.1 Deliver Consistent Messaging Across Channels

Whether a customer is engaging with your brand on Instagram, receiving an email in their inbox, or visiting your website, your messaging should be consistent and complementary. Use the following tips to ensure consistency:

- **Unified Tone and Voice**: Keep your brand voice and tone consistent across all channels to build familiarity and trust.
- **Integrated Campaigns**: Run coordinated campaigns that span across social media and email marketing, such as limited-time offers or product launches. Your social media posts can tease an email campaign, and your emails can remind customers to take action on social media.
- **Retargeting**: Use retargeting ads on Facebook, Instagram, and X for customers who have interacted with your emails or visited your website. Retargeting helps remind them about your brand and keeps your business top of mind.

## 3.2 Optimize the Customer Journey

Each customer's journey is unique, so it's important to tailor their experience based on where they are in the buying process. Your CRM can help track interactions and provide insights into what actions to take next.

- **Lead Nurturing**: Use email sequences and social media touchpoints to guide leads from awareness to consideration and ultimately to conversion.
- **Customer Retention**: Once someone has made a purchase, keep the relationship going by sending personalized follow-up emails, promoting loyalty programs, or sharing valuable content on social media.

- **Customer Feedback**: Use both email surveys and social media polls to gather feedback from your customers. This helps you improve your products, services, and overall experience.

## Step 4: Measure and Optimize Results

The key to creating an efficient and effective marketing strategy is continuous improvement. Use analytics and data from social media, email marketing, and CRM tools to measure your efforts and optimize accordingly.

### 4.1 Social Media Analytics

Monitor your social media performance using platform analytics (Instagram Insights, Facebook Analytics, X Analytics). Track metrics such as engagement, reach, click-through rate, and conversions. Use these insights to refine your social media content and targeting strategies.

### 4.2 Email Marketing Metrics

Monitor email marketing metrics like open rates, click-through rates, bounce rates, and unsubscribe rates. If certain types of emails aren't performing well, consider testing different subject lines, CTAs, or email designs.

### 4.3 CRM Reporting

Your CRM tool will offer reports on customer activity, engagement, and sales. Use this data to adjust your segmentation strategies, optimize automated workflows, and track the effectiveness of your overall marketing strategy.

## Wrapping Up

By combining social media, email marketing, and CRM tools, you can create a seamless, integrated customer experience that nurtures leads and drives conversions. This approach allows you to deliver personalized content at scale, ensuring your audience receives consistent messaging and relevant offers across all touchpoints. With the right tools and strategies, you can turn your social media followers into loyal customers and grow your business in a sustainable way.

# Chapter 19: How AI Can Help You Create Personal, Handwritten-Like Letters

In today's digital age, where automated emails and text messages have become the norm, a handwritten note stands out as one of the most personal and thoughtful ways to connect with someone. Whether you're expressing gratitude, building a relationship, or reaching out to prospects, a handwritten note conveys a level of care and sincerity that digital communication simply can't match. However, writing dozens—or even hundreds—of handwritten notes can be time-consuming, especially for busy professionals. That's where AI comes in.

With advances in AI technology, you can now upload your handwriting, and using AI tools, create handwritten-like notes that maintain the personal touch without the time investment. In this chapter, we'll explore the importance of handwritten notes in business relationships and how you can use AI to streamline this process and still have the feeling of a personal touch.

## Why Handwritten Notes Matter

Handwritten notes are an excellent way to make a memorable impression on your clients, prospects, or colleagues. Here's why they matter:

1. **Personal Connection**: A handwritten note makes the recipient feel special. It shows you took the time and effort to write something personal. This simple gesture goes a long way in building trust and rapport.
2. **Standing Out**: In a world full of emails and automated messages, a handwritten note stands out. It's a rare, memorable form of communication that people appreciate because it's not often seen anymore.
3. **Express Gratitude and Appreciation**: Whether it's thanking a client for their business or following up after a successful meeting, handwritten notes allow you to convey gratitude in a way that feels genuine and thoughtful.
4. **Enhancing Relationships**: Handwritten notes are great for building strong relationships with clients, prospects, and partners. They can be used to mark significant milestones, like anniversaries, closings, or birthdays, helping you stay top-of-mind and maintain a personal connection.

## How AI Can Create Handwritten-Like Notes

While you may want to send handwritten notes for that personal touch, writing each one by hand takes time—time that could be better spent focusing on other critical tasks. This is where AI technology can help. With the help of modern tools, you can upload your handwriting and create professional, handwritten-like notes in just a few clicks. Here's how it works:

### 1. Uploading Your Handwriting

There are AI tools and platforms that allow you to upload a sample of your handwriting—such as a scanned image or photo of a handwritten note. These tools then analyze your handwriting and replicate it with high precision. Some popular tools that offer this service include:

- **Handwritten AI**: This tool allows you to upload your handwriting to create personalized handwritten letters in a variety of styles and sizes. You can input text digitally, and the software will render it in a font that mirrors your handwriting.

- **LetterHound**: This AI-powered platform helps you generate personalized notes that look like your own handwriting. You simply upload a sample of your writing, and it will replicate the style in a digital format.

## 2. Customizing Your Handwritten Notes

Once your handwriting is uploaded, most of these AI tools give you the option to customize the note by adjusting elements like:

- **Font Style and Size**: You can choose a size and style that best matches the personal flair you want to project.
- **Ink Type**: Many tools offer a variety of ink types (e.g., blue, black, or even pencil) to make the note feel more authentic.
- **Paper Texture and Style**: Select from different types of paper or textures (e.g., parchment or lined paper) to give your note the perfect finish.

Once you've made these adjustments, the AI tool will generate a handwritten-like note that can be printed, mailed, or digitally sent to your recipient.

## 3. Scaling the Process

This is where AI truly saves time. Rather than writing each note by hand, AI allows you to scale the process. For example, you can write 100 personalized notes in a fraction of the time it would take to do them manually, while still maintaining the appearance and feel of a handwritten letter. It's a great way to stay engaged with clients and prospects without sacrificing your time.

## 4. Printing and Mailing

Once the note is generated, you can have it printed and mailed, or you can send it digitally. Many services will even send the note directly to your client or prospect via mail for you, further automating the process. This means you can still add that personal touch with minimal effort.

## Get Real: Using Handwritten-Like Notes in Real Estate

As a real estate professional, building strong relationships with clients, prospects, and partners is essential. In real estate, a personal touch can make a big difference, whether you're following up with potential buyers or thanking a client after closing on a home. Handwritten notes can be a powerful tool to enhance your business and build trust. Here's how you can apply AI-generated handwritten notes in real estate:

1. **Thanking Clients After a Closing**: Once your clients close on their new home, send them a personalized handwritten note expressing your gratitude for their trust and business. Use AI to generate the note quickly and efficiently, and add a personal touch by referencing specific details about their new home.

2. **Building Relationships with Prospects**: After meeting a prospect at an open house or initial consultation, follow up with a handwritten note thanking them for their time and interest. AI-generated handwritten notes can help you scale this process, allowing you to send personalized follow-ups to dozens of prospects without the time commitment.

3. **Congratulating Clients on Milestones**: Real estate is a relationship-driven industry, and celebrating your clients' milestones can help strengthen your connection. Use AI to send handwritten-like notes for birthdays, anniversaries, or the anniversary of their home purchase.

4. **Referral Appreciation**: Clients who refer their friends and family are incredibly valuable. Show your appreciation with a handwritten note, thanking them for the referral. This personal touch can help turn one-time clients into lifelong advocates.

5. **Staying Top-of-Mind**: Sending regular handwritten-like notes to clients and prospects, even when you don't have immediate business, can help keep you top-of-mind. A simple "thinking of you" or "hope all is well in your new home" note can go a long way in building long-term relationships.

## Wrapping Up

In an increasingly automated world, handwritten notes continue to be one of the most effective ways to connect on a personal level. AI allows you to scale this personal touch by generating handwritten-like notes quickly and efficiently. Whether you're a busy real estate professional or a business owner in any industry, using AI to replicate your handwriting can save you time while still providing your clients and prospects with the thoughtful, personal touch they'll remember.

# Chapter 20: Directory of AI-Powered CRMs

AI-powered Customer Relationship Management (CRM) systems leverage artificial intelligence to streamline business operations, enhance customer experience, and automate repetitive tasks. Here's a list of CRM platforms that integrate AI capabilities to optimize customer interactions, automate workflows, and provide actionable insights:

---

## 1. HubSpot CRM

- **AI Features**:
  - Predictive lead scoring
  - Chatbots for lead qualification and customer support
  - Smart email marketing and content recommendations
  - AI-powered reporting and analytics
- **Overview**: HubSpot is a widely popular CRM that offers AI-powered tools for automation, lead generation, and analytics. It's known for its ease of use and integration with other marketing tools, making it a solid choice for small to medium-sized businesses.
- **Best for**: Small and medium-sized businesses looking for an all-in-one marketing and CRM platform.

## 2. Salesforce Einstein

- **AI Features**:
  - Predictive analytics for sales forecasting
  - Personalized marketing and customer experiences
  - Lead and opportunity scoring
  - AI-powered chatbot and automation
- **Overview**: Salesforce Einstein is an AI-powered suite built directly into Salesforce CRM, offering deep data insights, predictive analytics, and automation. It helps businesses tailor customer interactions and improve sales productivity.
- **Best for**: Enterprises and large organizations seeking advanced CRM and AI capabilities.

---

## 3. Zoho CRM

- **AI Features**:
  - Zia AI assistant for lead scoring, email sentiment analysis, and sales forecasting
  - AI-driven workflows for task automation
  - Chatbot for customer interaction
  - Predictive analytics for smarter decision-making
- **Overview**: Zoho CRM offers AI through its Zia assistant, which helps sales teams make data-driven decisions, engage with customers, and automate repetitive tasks. It's suitable for businesses of all sizes and integrates well with other Zoho tools.
- **Best for**: Small to mid-sized businesses looking for a flexible, AI-powered CRM with automation.

---

## 4. Pipedrive

- **AI Features**:
  - Sales assistant AI for task management
  - AI-powered lead scoring and forecasting
  - Smart email templates with automated follow-ups
- **Overview**: Pipedrive is an intuitive CRM with AI features that help sales teams track and manage their pipeline, improve forecasting accuracy, and automate follow-up actions. It's designed to streamline sales processes and increase conversion rates.
- **Best for**: Sales-driven teams and small businesses that need a simple but effective CRM.

---

### 5. Freshsales (by Freshworks)

- **AI Features**:
  - Freddy AI assistant for lead scoring, predictive sales insights, and task automation
  - AI-powered email recommendations
  - Lead and opportunity management with AI-powered suggestions
- **Overview**: Freshsales offers Freddy AI to help businesses automate lead management, sales forecasting, and customer follow-ups. It's user-friendly and integrates with Freshworks' suite of customer support tools.
- **Best for**: SMBs that need a user-friendly CRM with integrated AI capabilities for lead management.

---

### 6. Insightly

- **AI Features**:
  - Predictive analytics for customer engagement
  - Lead scoring based on customer behavior
  - Automated task assignment and reminders

- **Overview**: Insightly is a CRM that integrates AI-driven features like predictive analytics to help users identify high-value leads and automate processes. It's particularly useful for project-driven businesses.
- **Best for**: Mid-sized businesses or project-based companies that need CRM and project management integration.

---

## 7. Creatio

- **AI Features**:
  - AI-driven marketing automation
  - Predictive lead scoring and sales insights
  - Chatbots and virtual assistants
  - Process mining for workflow optimization
- **Overview**: Creatio combines CRM with business process management and AI-driven marketing and sales automation. It's known for its flexibility, helping businesses design tailored workflows that improve customer interactions.
- **Best for**: Businesses with complex workflows and a need for customizable AI features.

---

## 8. Nimble

- **AI Features**:
  - Smart contacts and relationship management through AI-based insights
  - Social media and email engagement tracking
  - Predictive lead and sales forecasting
- **Overview**: Nimble is a CRM that focuses on relationship-building through AI-driven insights. It integrates with social media and emails to give you a 360-degree view of your relationships and automates tasks to keep your pipeline moving.

- **Best for**: Small businesses or solopreneurs who want an easy-to-use CRM for social selling and relationship management.

---

## 9. Monday.com

- **AI Features**:
  - AI-driven project and task management
  - Automated workflows with AI suggestions
  - Predictive analytics and task prioritization
- **Overview**: While Monday.com is primarily a work management platform, it offers CRM functionalities with AI features like task automation, workflow optimization, and predictive analytics to enhance project and customer relationship management.
- **Best for**: Teams that need a CRM integrated with project management features and advanced AI workflows.

---

## 10. Keap (formerly Infusionsoft)

- **AI Features**:
  - AI-driven lead scoring and follow-ups
  - Automated email campaigns based on customer behavior
  - Predictive insights for sales performance
- **Overview**: Keap is a CRM designed for small businesses with powerful automation and AI tools. It helps users automate customer outreach, manage leads, and improve sales performance through predictive insights and workflows.
- **Best for**: Small businesses or entrepreneurs looking for a CRM with strong automation and AI for sales processes.

---

## 11. Agile CRM

- **AI Features**:
    - AI-powered email campaigns with smart scheduling and content optimization
    - Predictive analytics for sales tracking and forecasting
    - Lead scoring and segmentation
- **Overview**: Agile CRM is a simple, easy-to-use CRM that includes AI-driven tools for lead scoring, email campaign automation, and analytics. It's designed to help small businesses grow by streamlining customer engagement.
- **Best for**: Small businesses looking for an affordable, easy-to-use CRM with AI capabilities.

---

## 12. SugarCRM

- **AI Features**:
    - AI-driven sales forecasting and predictive analytics
    - Smart recommendations and workflows for sales teams
    - Automation of routine tasks and email follow-ups
- **Overview**: SugarCRM's AI features, known as SugarPredict, help businesses analyze customer data, forecast sales, and improve customer engagement by providing actionable insights and automating processes.
- **Best for**: Mid-sized to large businesses looking for an enterprise-level CRM with AI-driven insights.

---

# Get Real: Using AI-Powered CRMs in Real Estate

In real estate, managing relationships with clients and leads is crucial to success. From first-time homebuyers to seasoned investors, each client has different needs, preferences, and timelines. Leveraging AI-powered CRM systems can help real estate professionals stay organized, personalize their outreach, and ultimately close more deals. Here's how AI-driven CRMs, including Follow Up Boss and others, can be applied specifically to real estate:

---

## 1. Follow Up Boss

- **AI Features**:
    - Automated lead assignment and follow-up reminders
    - Predictive lead scoring based on engagement levels
    - SMS and email automation for client follow-ups
    - Custom workflows for streamlined communications
- **How It Helps in Real Estate**: Follow Up Boss is specifically designed for real estate professionals, and its AI features are great for managing leads, tracking communications, and ensuring timely follow-ups. With automated follow-up reminders, you'll never miss an opportunity, and predictive lead scoring helps you prioritize high-quality leads. In real estate, where quick responses can make all the difference, Follow Up Boss ensures you're always ahead of the game.

**Real-World Application**:

- **Lead Management**: When a new lead comes in—whether from an open house, online ad, or referral—Follow Up Boss automatically assigns the lead to the right agent and sends an instant follow-up email or text. This instant response is crucial in a fast-paced market.
- **Client Engagement**: The AI helps track how engaged clients are with your communications (open rates,

responses, etc.) and adjusts your outreach accordingly. For instance, if a lead hasn't responded to emails, the system will prompt you to send a more personalized message, helping increase conversion rates.

---

## 2. BoomTown

- **AI Features**:
    - Automated lead scoring and lead nurturing
    - Predictive analytics for client behavior and engagement
    - Drip email campaigns for continuous communication
    - Behavioral tracking across all digital channels
- **How It Helps in Real Estate**: BoomTown uses AI to help agents prioritize high-value leads and automate much of the initial lead nurturing process. The platform's predictive capabilities track a lead's activity across multiple touchpoints (website, email, social media) to determine the right time for a follow-up. In the competitive world of real estate, timing is critical, and BoomTown's AI ensures that you reach out to leads at just the right moment.

**Real-World Application**:

- **Automated Follow-ups**: BoomTown's AI automates follow-ups based on lead behavior, meaning you can focus on other tasks while it nurtures leads who might be in the research phase.
- **Lead Scoring**: It assigns a score to each lead based on their activity and likelihood to convert, ensuring that agents spend their time with leads that are most likely to close.

---

## 3. LionDesk

- **AI Features**:
  - Automated email, text, and video messaging
  - AI-powered chatbots for instant lead responses
  - Predictive lead scoring and activity tracking
  - Drip campaigns and automated follow-ups
- **How It Helps in Real Estate**: LionDesk's AI-powered features make it easy for real estate agents to stay in touch with clients and leads across multiple channels. With its text, email, and video message automation, agents can save time while still providing personalized communication. AI-powered chatbots can also engage leads 24/7, capturing information and qualifying leads while you sleep.

**Real-World Application**:

- **Chatbots for Lead Qualification**: LionDesk's chatbots can answer questions on your website or through text, qualifying leads and scheduling appointments automatically. This ensures that no lead goes cold while waiting for an agent to respond.
- **Automated Drip Campaigns**: For leads in the research phase, LionDesk automates drip campaigns to stay top of mind. AI monitors lead activity and adjusts the campaign to nurture them towards a buying decision.

---

### 4. KVCore

- **AI Features**:
  - Smart CRM with AI-powered lead management
  - Behavioral tracking for predictive insights
  - Automated follow-ups and reminders
  - AI-powered marketing tools like email and social media campaigns
- **How It Helps in Real Estate**: KVCore is a powerful AI-driven platform tailored for real estate agents. Its lead management tools use AI to identify the most promising leads based on their activity and engagement. The

system automatically sends follow-ups and reminders, reducing the need for manual input. Plus, KVCore's marketing tools, such as automated social media posts and email campaigns, ensure your content reaches the right people at the right time.

**Real-World Application**:

- **Predictive Lead Insights**: KVCore's AI tracks a lead's behavior and uses predictive analytics to gauge when they are most likely to convert. This allows agents to focus their efforts on the hottest leads and engage with them at the optimal time.
- **Automated Marketing**: With KVCore, you can automate everything from Facebook ads to email newsletters, ensuring your content reaches leads consistently without the need for constant manual input.

## 5. Top Producer

- **AI Features**:
    - Predictive lead scoring and activity tracking
    - Automated follow-up tasks and reminders
    - AI-powered email marketing campaigns
    - Real-time lead notifications
- **How It Helps in Real Estate**: Top Producer offers AI-powered tools for managing leads and contacts, ensuring that agents can respond quickly and stay organized. The platform's AI helps prioritize high-value leads and prompts agents when it's time to follow up. With automated email campaigns, agents can stay engaged with their clients without needing to manually write emails every time.

**Real-World Application**:

- **Automated Communication**: Agents can automate emails for new listings, open houses, and price reductions. Top Producer's AI ensures these communications are sent to the right leads at the right time.

- **Smart Reminders**: The system sends reminders based on lead activity and engagement, helping agents follow up on opportunities without relying on memory.

## How to Leverage AI-Powered CRMs in Real Estate: Key Takeaways

1. **Automated Lead Nurturing**: Real estate CRMs with AI can automate the follow-up process, sending personalized messages and reminders at just the right moment. This ensures no lead goes forgotten.
2. **Prioritize High-Value Leads**: AI-driven lead scoring helps you focus on the hottest leads, optimizing your time and efforts. Leads who are actively engaging with your content or showing interest in your services will be identified early.
3. **Behavior-Driven Engagement**: AI tracks lead behavior and triggers automatic responses based on actions like website visits, email opens, or form submissions. This makes your communication timely and relevant.
4. **Scalable Follow-Up**: Using AI to send automatic follow-up emails, texts, and even video messages means you can engage with a larger pool of clients without compromising the personal touch. Automated drip campaigns nurture leads over time, moving them down the funnel.
5. **Better Insights and Decisions**: AI analyzes customer interactions and provides you with data-driven insights that help you make better decisions. From predictive sales forecasts to understanding which content is performing best, AI makes sure you're always operating with accurate, real-time information.

## In Summary

In real estate, staying organized, responsive, and efficient is critical to success. AI-powered CRMs like Follow Up Boss, BoomTown, LionDesk, KVCore, and Top Producer are game-changers in helping agents automate communication, prioritize high-value leads, and nurture relationships. These tools allow you to engage clients on a deeper level without overwhelming yourself with administrative tasks. With the right AI CRM, you can scale your business, close more deals, and maintain lasting relationships with your clients.

In the next chapter, we'll explore how AI can further enhance your marketing strategies and help you automate the creation of content that speaks to your audience.

# Chapter 21: AI Tools for Creating Content

Creating engaging, high-quality content can be time-consuming, but with the help of AI tools, you can streamline the process, generate ideas, and produce content that resonates with your audience. Here's a list of AI-powered tools that can help with various aspects of content creation:

---

## 1. ChatGPT by OpenAI

- **Features**:
    - AI-generated text for blogs, articles, social media posts, and more
    - Natural language processing to mimic human writing style
    - Idea generation for content topics and headlines
- **Best For**: Content writing, ideation, and conversational content (e.g., customer service chatbots).

---

## 2. Jasper (formerly Jarvis)

- **Features**:
    - AI copywriting for ads, blogs, emails, product descriptions, and social posts
    - Content templates for quick generation (e.g., blog intros, social media posts)

- Tone and style customization
- **Best For**: Businesses that need high-quality, scalable content for marketing, ads, and blogs.

---

## 3. Copy.ai

- **Features**:
  - AI-powered content generation for headlines, social media captions, blog posts, and product descriptions
  - Templates and customizable output
  - Ability to write in multiple languages
- **Best For**: Small businesses and marketers who need to generate copy quickly and effectively.

---

## 4. Writesonic

- **Features**:
  - AI-assisted writing for articles, blogs, emails, and more
  - AI-generated content for SEO optimization
  - Long-form and short-form content generation
- **Best For**: Content marketers, SEO specialists, and businesses looking to scale their content output.

---

## 5. Frase

- **Features**:
  - AI-driven content creation and SEO optimization
  - Generates high-ranking articles based on targeted keywords
  - Content research and AI writing assistant tools

- **Best For**: Content marketers, bloggers, and SEO experts focused on creating search-engine-optimized content.

---

## 6. Rytr

- **Features**:
    - AI-generated content for blog posts, email campaigns, ads, and more
    - Content templates for different niches (e.g., eCommerce, real estate, health)
    - Multi-language support for global content creation
- **Best For**: Solopreneurs, small businesses, and teams that need content creation across different channels.

---

## 7. QuillBot

- **Features**:
    - Paraphrasing tool powered by AI to rewrite content
    - Grammar and style improvements
    - Summarization and citation features
- **Best For**: Content creators looking to rephrase, enhance, or condense existing content.

---

## 8. Piktochart

- **Features**:
    - AI-assisted design tools for creating infographics, presentations, and reports
    - Easy drag-and-drop editor with templates
    - Data visualization tools powered by AI

- **Best For**: Marketers, educators, and businesses needing visual content like infographics and presentations.

---

## 9. Lumen5

- **Features**:
  - AI-powered video creation from blog posts or text content
  - Automatic scene selection and music recommendations
  - Customizable video templates
- **Best For**: Content creators looking to turn written content into engaging videos for social media or marketing purposes.

---

## 10. Wordtune

- **Features**:
  - AI-powered writing assistant to improve tone, style, and readability
  - Rewriting, shortening, and expanding content
  - Multi-language support
- **Best For**: Writers and content creators who want to refine their content for clarity, tone, and engagement.

---

## 11. Scalenut

- **Features**:
  - AI-driven content creation and SEO research tools
  - Content briefs, keyword analysis, and topic suggestions
  - Long-form content creation with AI assistance

- **Best For**: Businesses focused on creating SEO-optimized, long-form content like blog posts and articles.

## 12. INK Editor

- **Features**:
  - AI-powered content optimization for SEO
  - Real-time content scoring for keyword density and SEO ranking
  - AI content suggestions to improve readability and engagement
- **Best For**: Content creators and marketers focusing on high-visibility content for search engines.

## 13. ContentBot

- **Features**:
  - AI-powered content generation for blog posts, email campaigns, and more
  - SEO optimization and long-form content writing
  - Idea generation for blog topics and headlines
- **Best For**: Content marketers looking to scale content production and optimize it for SEO.

## 14. Article Forge

- **Features**:
  - AI-driven long-form content generation
  - Automatic article writing based on a given keyword or topic
  - Content creation designed to mimic human writing style
- **Best For**: Businesses or individuals needing fast, high-quality articles for blogs or websites.

## 15. AdZis

- **Features**:
  - AI-powered content creation for eCommerce businesses
  - Product descriptions, ad copy, and other marketing content generation
  - Customizable templates for different product categories
- **Best For**: eCommerce businesses needing high-volume product descriptions and ad copy.

## 16. Kuki Chatbot

- **Features**:
  - AI-powered chatbot for generating conversational content
  - Personalized responses and customer interaction
  - Automated lead qualification through AI-driven conversations
- **Best For**: Businesses looking for AI-powered customer service or lead generation through chatbots.

# Conclusion

These AI-powered content creation tools can help you streamline the writing process, improve efficiency, and produce high-quality content across multiple formats. Whether you're a small business owner, content marketer, or creative professional, these tools can help you generate blog posts, social media updates, video scripts, product descriptions, and much more. By integrating AI into your content strategy, you can save time, increase productivity, and create engaging content that resonates with your target audience.

# Chapter 22: Increase Productivity with Autoclickers

## 1. Fast Mouse Clicker

- **Features**:
    - Simple, lightweight auto-clicking tool
    - Allows for customizable click rates (click speed)
    - Supports left and right mouse buttons
- **Best For**: Basic auto-clicking tasks such as games or repetitive actions.

## 2. GS Auto Clicker

- **Features**:
    - Easy-to-use interface for setting up automated clicks
    - Customizable hotkeys to start/stop clicking
    - Adjustable click intervals and repeat counts
- **Best For**: Users who need a straightforward tool with minimal setup.

## 3. AutoClicker by Shocker

- **Features**:
    - Multiple click modes (single, double, or multi-click)
    - Adjustable speed and interval times

- Lightweight and no installation required (portable version available)
- **Best For**: Those looking for flexibility in the clicking process and no installation.

## 4. TinyTask

- **Features**:
  - Macro recording for automating repetitive tasks
  - Allows you to record a sequence of actions and playback automatically
  - Very lightweight and easy to use
- **Best For**: Users who need automation beyond simple clicking (e.g., keyboard and mouse actions combined).

## 5. AutoHotkey

- **Features**:
  - A powerful scripting tool that allows you to write custom scripts for automation, including auto-clicking
  - Fully customizable (can automate mouse, keyboard, and other tasks)
  - Great for advanced users who want complete control over the automation process
- **Best For**: Advanced users looking for deep customization and flexibility.

## 6. OP Auto Clicker

- **Features**:
  - Supports both single and double-click options
  - Allows you to set the interval between clicks
  - Customizable hotkeys for starting and stopping
- **Best For**: Users who need a simple, reliable auto-clicker for basic tasks.

## 7. Free Auto Clicker

- **Features**:
  - Simple, no-frills auto-clicking tool
  - Allows you to set the frequency of clicks
  - Adjustable click button (left, right, or middle click)
- **Best For**: Casual users who need an easy-to-use, free tool for basic clicking tasks.

## 8. Auto Clicker Typer

- **Features**:
  - Capable of both mouse clicks and keyboard typing automation
  - Customizable interval for clicks and typing speed
  - Lightweight and easy to configure
- **Best For**: Those looking to automate both mouse and keyboard actions, useful for gaming or data entry tasks.

## 9. PTFB Pro (Push The Freakin' Button Pro)

- **Features**:
  - Allows for automation of mouse clicks and key presses
  - Advanced features for users needing specific triggers for clicks
  - Option to schedule clicks at specific times or intervals
- **Best For**: Users who need more advanced features for controlling complex automation tasks.

## 10. AutoClicker 1.0

- **Features**:
  - Allows users to automate single or double-clicking at set intervals
  - Hotkey activation for starting/stopping auto-clicking
  - Simple interface and easy setup
- **Best For**: Those seeking an uncomplicated tool for basic mouse automation.

## 11. Clickermann

- **Features**:
    - Automated mouse clicking with advanced timing controls
    - Customizable hotkeys
    - Supports left, right, and middle-click
- **Best For**: People looking for precision and control over their clicking automation.

## 12. Macro Recorder

- **Features**:
    - Records mouse movements and clicks as macros
    - Can automate repetitive tasks such as clicking and dragging
    - Offers playback, customization, and scheduling of macros
- **Best For**: Users needing a comprehensive automation tool for both keyboard and mouse tasks.

---

## Important Note:

Using auto-clickers in some contexts (e.g., games or online platforms) can violate terms of service and result in penalties or bans. Always ensure that you are using auto-clickers in accordance with the rules of the platform you are engaging with.

These auto-clicker tools can be incredibly helpful for automating repetitive tasks, improving productivity, and saving time across various industries, including gaming, data entry, and marketing automation.

# Chapter 23 : Where to Get Your Website: Top Platforms for Building Your Online Presence

In today's digital age, having a professional website is essential for any business, personal brand, or creative project. Whether you're an entrepreneur looking to showcase your products, a blogger sharing your insights, or a creative building an online portfolio, choosing the right platform to create your website is the first step to success. In this chapter, we'll explore the top platforms to help you get started, along with their unique features to suit different needs.

---

**1. Wix: The All-in-One Website Builder**

Wix is one of the most popular website builders, known for its user-friendly interface and flexibility. It offers:

- **Drag-and-Drop Interface**: You don't need to know any code to create a website on Wix. The intuitive drag-and-drop editor lets you customize designs easily.

- **Template Variety**: Choose from hundreds of templates across industries like e-commerce, blogs, photography, and more.
- **Add-Ons and Integrations**: Wix supports a range of add-ons for SEO, social media integration, and e-commerce tools.
- **Pricing**: Offers a free version with basic features, and paid plans for more advanced features and custom domains.

*Best For*: Beginners, small businesses, and personal websites.

---

## 2. WordPress: The Powerhouse of Customization

WordPress is the world's most widely used website platform, powering over 40% of websites on the internet. It's highly customizable and perfect for those who need more control over their site's design and functionality.

- **Themes and Plugins**: Choose from thousands of themes and plugins to create a website that fits your exact needs, from blogs to e-commerce stores.
- **Open-Source**: WordPress is open-source, meaning there's a large community of developers constantly creating new features and updates.
- **SEO-Friendly**: WordPress is designed with SEO in mind, helping your website rank better on search engines.
- **Pricing**: WordPress itself is free, but you'll need to pay for hosting and a custom domain.

*Best For*: Bloggers, businesses, and anyone who wants full control over their website's customization.

---

## 3. Squarespace: Sleek and Professional Design

Squarespace is known for its beautiful and professionally designed templates, making it a top choice for creatives and businesses that prioritize design.

- **Design-Centric Templates**: Squarespace's templates are modern, responsive, and customizable, with a strong emphasis on aesthetics.
- **Built-In Tools**: Features such as e-commerce tools, blogging functionality, and marketing integrations are built right into the platform.
- **Ease of Use**: The drag-and-drop editor is easy to navigate, and the platform handles all the technical details, so you can focus on content.
- **Pricing**: Squarespace offers various pricing plans based on the features you need, with a free trial available.

*Best For:* Artists, photographers, small businesses, and anyone seeking visually stunning websites.

---

### 4. Shopify: The E-Commerce Specialist

If you're looking to build an online store, Shopify is a go-to platform for building e-commerce websites. It's designed to help you sell products easily and scale your online business.

- **E-Commerce Tools**: Shopify provides all the features you need to run an online store, including inventory management, payment processing, and shipping integrations.
- **Templates and Customization**: Choose from over 70 professional themes or customize your store's design to your liking.
- **App Integrations**: Shopify has an extensive app store, offering additional tools for marketing, sales, and customer support.
- **Pricing**: Shopify offers several pricing tiers depending on the features you need, with a free trial available.

*Best For:* Entrepreneurs and businesses looking to sell products online.

---

### 5. Weebly: Easy-to-Use for Beginners

Weebly is another beginner-friendly website builder that offers a drag-and-drop editor with a simple interface, making it easy for anyone to build a website quickly.

- **Drag-and-Drop Interface**: No technical skills are needed to build a site with Weebly's simple drag-and-drop editor.
- **E-Commerce Features**: Weebly also offers e-commerce tools, such as product listings, online payments, and inventory tracking.
- **Mobile-Friendly**: The platform automatically makes your website mobile-responsive, ensuring it looks great on all devices.
- **Pricing**: Weebly offers a free plan, with additional premium features available through paid subscriptions.

*Best For:* Beginners and small businesses looking for a simple, cost-effective solution.

---

### 6. Webflow: Advanced Design and Customization

Webflow is a platform that bridges the gap between traditional website builders and full-on custom coding. It's perfect for users who want more creative control but still prefer a visual design interface.

- **Custom Design**: Webflow offers more control over your website's design than most builders, allowing you to create unique layouts and animations.
- **Responsive Design**: It automatically generates responsive websites, ensuring they look good on all devices.

- **CMS and E-Commerce**: Webflow includes content management and e-commerce features, making it ideal for businesses with dynamic content.
- **Pricing**: Webflow offers free basic websites, but more advanced features and hosting come with premium plans.

*Best For:* Designers and developers who want full creative control without writing code.

---

## 7. GoDaddy Website Builder: Quick and Simple

GoDaddy is known for its domain registration services, but it also offers a website builder that allows you to get a website up and running in no time.

- **Simple Setup**: With GoDaddy's builder, you can create a website in just a few clicks, with an easy setup wizard guiding you through the process.
- **Mobile-Optimized**: All sites created on GoDaddy's builder are automatically mobile-friendly.
- **Integrated Marketing Tools**: The platform includes built-in email marketing, SEO, and social media tools to help grow your online presence.
- **Pricing**: GoDaddy offers various pricing plans, with a free trial and affordable paid plans.

*Best For:* Small businesses, entrepreneurs, and individuals looking for a simple, fast solution.

---

## 8. BigCommerce: Scalable E-Commerce for Growing Businesses

BigCommerce is an e-commerce platform that's ideal for growing businesses that need more advanced tools to scale.

- **Scalable E-Commerce Solutions**: BigCommerce provides a powerful platform for scaling businesses, with advanced tools for product management, shipping, and analytics.
- **Multichannel Selling**: It allows you to sell on various platforms, including Amazon, eBay, Facebook, and Instagram, all from a single dashboard.
- **SEO and Marketing Tools**: BigCommerce is built with SEO in mind, and includes built-in marketing tools like email campaigns and discounts.
- **Pricing**: BigCommerce offers a range of pricing plans based on the size of your business and the features you need.

*Best For*: Growing businesses looking for a comprehensive e-commerce solution.

---

## Conclusion: Finding the Right Platform for Your Needs

Choosing the right platform to build your website depends on your goals, budget, and technical abilities. Whether you're looking for an easy-to-use website builder, a powerful e-commerce solution, or a highly customizable platform, there's a website provider that fits your needs. Start by identifying your priorities—whether that's design, e-commerce, or simplicity—and select a platform that aligns with your vision. Once your website is up and running, you can begin creating valuable content and building your online presence, making your mark in the digital world.

# Chapter: Building Your Online Storefront: The Best Tools for E-Commerce Success

Creating an online store is a crucial step for entrepreneurs looking to sell products and services in the digital world. Whether you're launching a small boutique or scaling a large online business, the right tools can help you set up a professional, user-friendly storefront. In this chapter, we'll explore the best online storefront creation tools that offer various features for customization, payment processing, inventory management, and marketing, so you can choose the platform that best suits your business needs.

---

### 1. Shopify: The E-Commerce Giant

Shopify is one of the most well-known e-commerce platforms and for good reason. It's an all-in-one solution designed to help businesses of all sizes create an online store with ease.

- **Ease of Use**: Shopify offers a user-friendly drag-and-drop interface, making it accessible even for beginners.
- **Customization**: With a wide range of themes and apps, Shopify allows you to fully customize your store's design and functionality.
- **Payment Integration**: Shopify integrates with multiple payment gateways and provides its own Shopify Payments service for easier transactions.
- **E-Commerce Tools**: Inventory management, product variations, and marketing tools (like discounts, email marketing, and abandoned cart recovery) come built-in.
- **Pricing**: Shopify offers tiered pricing plans, from a basic plan for new stores to advanced solutions for large businesses. They also offer a 14-day free trial.

*Best For*: Entrepreneurs, small businesses, and large retailers looking for an all-in-one, scalable e-commerce solution.

## 2. BigCommerce: Ideal for Growing Businesses

BigCommerce is another powerful e-commerce platform that offers robust features for scaling your business. It's ideal for businesses looking for a more comprehensive solution to manage their storefront, products, and transactions.

- **Customizability**: BigCommerce allows for extensive customization and offers both a drag-and-drop editor and the ability to use HTML/CSS for advanced design options.
- **Multichannel Selling**: You can integrate your store with marketplaces like Amazon, eBay, Facebook, and Instagram, expanding your reach.
- **SEO & Marketing**: BigCommerce provides advanced SEO tools, email marketing, and abandoned cart recovery to optimize sales.
- **Advanced Reporting**: Get detailed insights into your sales performance and customer behavior to improve decision-making.
- **Pricing**: BigCommerce has different pricing tiers, with higher-tier plans offering more advanced features. There's also a 15-day free trial.

*Best For*: Medium to large businesses needing an advanced, scalable platform with multichannel capabilities.

## 3. WooCommerce: WordPress Integration for E-Commerce

WooCommerce is a free WordPress plugin that turns any WordPress site into a fully functional online store. It's one of the most popular e-commerce platforms for users who are already familiar with WordPress.

- **Customization**: As a WordPress plugin, WooCommerce allows you to access thousands of themes and plugins for limitless customization.

- **Open-Source**: WooCommerce is open-source, so developers can build custom features if needed.
- **Extensive Features**: Features like inventory management, shipping options, tax calculations, and multiple payment gateways are included.
- **Integration with WordPress**: If you already have a WordPress site, WooCommerce integrates seamlessly to add e-commerce functionality.
- **Pricing**: WooCommerce itself is free, but you may need to pay for hosting, premium themes, and additional plugins.

*Best For*: WordPress users who want an affordable and highly customizable e-commerce platform.

---

## 4. Squarespace: Simple and Elegant E-Commerce

Squarespace is well known for its beautiful, design-centric website templates, and its e-commerce functionality is just as polished. It's a great platform for small businesses and creatives who want a simple, elegant online store.

- **Beautiful Templates**: Squarespace's templates are sleek and mobile-optimized, perfect for visually-driven businesses like clothing, art, or photography.
- **Drag-and-Drop Builder**: The platform provides an easy-to-use editor to help you build your store without any coding.
- **Integrated E-Commerce Features**: Squarespace offers payment processing, inventory management, and order tracking, plus options for selling digital products.
- **Built-in Marketing Tools**: Use Squarespace's built-in email campaigns, social media integrations, and SEO tools to market your products.
- **Pricing**: Squarespace has pricing plans for both personal and business use, starting from a basic plan

with e-commerce features to more advanced options for larger stores.

*Best For:* Small businesses and creative entrepreneurs looking for a visually appealing, easy-to-manage online store.

---

### 5. Wix: A Flexible, Beginner-Friendly Option

Wix is another drag-and-drop website builder that offers e-commerce features for entrepreneurs who want a simple way to sell products online.

- **Ease of Use**: Wix's intuitive drag-and-drop interface makes it easy for beginners to set up their online store without technical skills.
- **Design Freedom**: Choose from a wide variety of templates and customize your store using the flexible design tools.
- **App Market**: Wix's app market provides additional functionalities like customer reviews, email marketing, and abandoned cart recovery.
- **Payment Options**: Wix supports multiple payment gateways, including PayPal and credit card processing.
- **Pricing**: Wix offers affordable pricing plans, with options for both personal websites and full-featured e-commerce stores. A free plan is available, but you'll need a premium plan for e-commerce.

*Best For:* Small businesses, creatives, and beginners who want a simple, cost-effective solution for selling products online.

---

### 6. Weebly: Simple E-Commerce for Beginners

Weebly is another easy-to-use website builder that includes built-in e-commerce tools. It's a great option for entrepreneurs who need to get their store up quickly and without hassle.

- **User-Friendly**: Weebly's drag-and-drop website builder is straightforward, allowing anyone to create a store without needing technical skills.
- **E-Commerce Features**: Basic e-commerce tools like inventory management, order tracking, and payment gateways are included in Weebly's plans.
- **Mobile-Optimized**: All Weebly stores are mobile-friendly, ensuring your products look great on smartphones and tablets.
- **Marketing Tools**: Weebly provides tools for SEO, email marketing, and social media integration to help grow your store.
- **Pricing**: Weebly offers a free plan with limited features, and paid plans are available for more advanced e-commerce tools.

*Best For*: Beginners and small businesses who want an affordable, no-fuss e-commerce store.

## Conclusion: Choosing the Right Storefront Creation Tool

When it comes to creating your online storefront, the right platform depends on your needs, level of experience, and business size. Whether you're a small business just starting out, a creative entrepreneur building a visually-driven store, or a growing e-commerce brand looking for advanced features, there's a platform that fits your goals. Evaluate your priorities—whether it's design, customization, scalability, or cost—and choose the tool that aligns with your vision. No matter which tool you choose, building a professional, easy-to-navigate online storefront will set the foundation for your e-commerce success.

# Glossary of Technical Terms

This glossary will help you understand the key technical terms used throughout the book, especially those related to AI, CRMs, digital marketing, and automation. Here's a breakdown of important concepts that will aid your understanding as you dive into how to use AI tools for business growth.

---

## A

- **AI (Artificial Intelligence)**: The simulation of human intelligence in machines that can perform tasks like learning, reasoning, and problem-solving. In business, AI is often used for automation, customer insights, and decision-making.
- **Automation**: The use of technology to perform tasks that would typically require human intervention, such as sending emails, following up with clients, or posting on social media.
- **API (Application Programming Interface)**: A set of tools and protocols that allow different software applications to communicate with each other. APIs are often used to integrate various AI tools or CRMs with other business systems.
- **Ad Copy**: The written content used in advertisements. It's designed to engage the audience and encourage a specific action, such as purchasing a product or clicking on a link.

---

## B

- **Behavioral Targeting**: A technique used in digital marketing where ads are tailored to users based on their past actions, such as browsing history or interactions with a website.

- **Boomerang Effect**: A situation where a marketing tactic that is meant to build engagement backfires and negatively impacts the business or campaign.
- **B2B (Business to Business)**: A business model where one company sells products or services to another business, rather than directly to consumers.
- **B2C (Business to Consumer)**: A business model where companies sell products or services directly to consumers.

---

## C

- **CRM (Customer Relationship Management)**: A technology platform used to manage a company's interactions with current and potential customers. It helps businesses track and manage customer data, communication, and relationships.
- **Chatbot**: An AI-powered tool that can simulate human conversation. Chatbots are commonly used on websites, social media, or in customer service to handle inquiries and automate tasks.
- **Click-Through Rate (CTR)**: A metric used in digital marketing to measure the percentage of users who click on a link or ad compared to the total number of users who viewed it.
- **Content Calendar**: A plan or schedule that outlines what content will be published and when, often used in marketing campaigns to stay organized.
- **Copywriting**: The act of writing persuasive text, typically for advertising or marketing purposes.

---

## D

- **Drip Campaign**: A type of email marketing campaign where a series of pre-written messages are sent automatically over time to nurture leads and guide them through the sales funnel.

- **Digital Marketing**: The use of online platforms and tools to promote products or services, including social media, email, search engines, and websites.
- **Deep Learning**: A subset of AI that mimics the human brain's neural networks, allowing computers to process and learn from large sets of data in more sophisticated ways.

---

# E

- **Email Automation**: The use of software to send targeted emails to customers automatically, based on predefined triggers like a customer's behavior or time of the day.
- **Engagement**: A measure of how actively a customer interacts with content, such as liking, commenting, sharing, or clicking on links.
- **E-commerce**: The buying and selling of products or services over the internet. E-commerce platforms often use AI to personalize shopping experiences and streamline processes like inventory management.

---

# F

- **Follow-Up**: A crucial step in sales and customer service, where businesses follow up with potential or existing customers to build relationships and move them through the sales pipeline.
- **Follow-Up Boss**: A CRM platform specifically designed for real estate professionals, which includes features like automated follow-ups, lead tracking, and integration with other tools.
- **Funnels**: A marketing concept that describes the customer journey from the first interaction to making a

purchase, often visualized as a funnel because many leads drop off before conversion.

---

# G

- **Google Analytics**: A tool that tracks and reports website traffic, helping businesses understand user behavior and make data-driven decisions for marketing strategies.
- **Gamification**: The application of game-design elements and principles in non-game contexts (like marketing) to increase engagement and encourage specific behaviors.

---

# H

- **Hot Leads**: Leads that show a strong interest in a product or service and are more likely to convert into paying customers.
- **Hashtag**: A word or phrase preceded by the "#" symbol, used on social media platforms to categorize content or make it easier to find.

---

# I

- **Inbound Marketing**: A marketing strategy focused on attracting customers through content and experiences that are relevant and helpful, rather than interruptive advertising.
- **Integrations**: The process of connecting different software tools (like CRMs, email marketing tools, and social media platforms) to work together seamlessly.
- **Influencer Marketing**: A form of marketing where businesses partner with influencers (people with a large

following on social media) to promote products or services.

- **Impressions**: A metric that measures the number of times an ad or piece of content is shown to a user.

---

# L

- **Lead Scoring**: A method of ranking leads based on their likelihood to convert, often using AI to analyze behavior, engagement, and demographic data.
- **Lead Nurturing**: The process of building relationships with potential customers over time, using targeted content, follow-ups, and personalized communication.

---

# M

- **Machine Learning**: A subset of AI where systems learn from data and improve their performance over time without being explicitly programmed.
- **Marketing Automation**: The use of software to automate marketing tasks such as emails, social media posts, and ad campaigns.
- **Metrics**: Quantitative measurements used to track the performance of marketing campaigns, such as conversion rates, CTR, and ROI.

---

# P

- **Predictive Analytics**: AI-based techniques that analyze data to predict future outcomes, helping businesses make data-driven decisions about lead generation, marketing, and sales.

- **Personalization**: Tailoring content, messages, or offers to an individual's preferences, behaviors, or demographics using AI.
- **Product Descriptions**: Text that explains the features, benefits, and uses of a product. AI can help generate optimized product descriptions for eCommerce websites.
- **Post Scheduling**: The process of planning and scheduling social media posts in advance using tools that automate the process.

## R

- **Real-Time Analytics**: Data analysis that happens as the events occur, providing businesses with up-to-the-minute insights on customer behavior and campaign performance.
- **Retargeting**: A form of online advertising that targets users who have previously interacted with a brand or visited its website.
- **ROI (Return on Investment)**: A measure used to evaluate the profitability of an investment, calculated by dividing the net profit by the cost of the investment.

## S

- **Segmentation**: The process of dividing a customer or lead list into smaller, targeted groups based on characteristics like demographics, behavior, or preferences.
- **SEO (Search Engine Optimization)**: The practice of optimizing content and websites to rank higher in search engine results pages, increasing organic traffic.
- **Social Proof**: The concept of using testimonials, reviews, or user-generated content to influence potential customers' purchasing decisions.

# T

- **Triggers**: Specific actions or behaviors that automatically initiate a response, such as sending a welcome email when someone subscribes to a newsletter.
- **Target Audience**: The specific group of people a business aims to reach with its marketing efforts, based on factors like demographics, interests, and buying behaviors.
- **Text Bots**: AI-powered tools that automate text messaging interactions, often used for customer service or sales purposes.

# V

- **Visual Content**: Any content that involves visual elements, such as images, videos, and infographics. AI tools like Lumen5 can assist in creating video content from written material.

This glossary provides a foundation for understanding the technical terms and concepts discussed in the book. As you explore AI tools and digital marketing strategies, these terms will help clarify how different technologies and techniques can work together to enhance your business operations.